IMAGINATION OF HEARTSTRING

Reza Abelechian

Printed By:
Book Writing Crew
Printed in the United States of America

First Printing Edition, 2024

ISBN: Paperback: 978-1-963258-17-2
Hardcover: 978-1-963258-18-9

Dedication

In the presence of God, whose divine guidance and unwavering love have been my source of strength and inspiration, I humbly offer my deepest gratitude.

For my beloved parents, your boundless love and unyielding support have been the cornerstone of my journey as a person. Your belief in me has been my guiding light.

With heartfelt appreciation for my cherished wife, your faith, patience, and understanding have breathed life into my creative aspirations. You are my muse and my greatest blessing.

To honour my dear sisters, your love, encouragement, unwavering support, and optimistic belief in my dreams have been a constant source of motivation and courage.

With immense gratitude to my precious family, your love, warmth, and unfaltering support have been my shelter in the storm, giving me the strength to pursue my passions.

In recognition of my dear friends, your earnest enthusiasm, encouragement, and unshakable notion of my talents have fueled my spirit and filled my days with joy.

This book is a testament to the love, faith, and support of each and every one of you. With heartfelt emotion, I dedicate this work to you, my guiding stars.

Author's Note

Contents

Introduction

Every day, an average of 6,000 thoughts dart through the human mind. Imagine if just one of those could spark a revolution of positivity. In a world where chaos often reigns, I invite you to a sanctuary of serenity, where optimism is not just a fleeting whisper but a resounding echo. Born amidst the rich tapestry of Iranian culture, tempered by the robust simplicity of Danish living, and now threading through London's vibrant pulse, I, Reza Abelechian, stand before you—a bridge between worlds, a businessman, a philanthropist, and now, a weaver of stories. Why, you might wonder, does this matter to you? Because within these pages lies the power to transform the mundane into the magnificent, to find solace in the storm, and to reimagine the fabric of reality. Can you recall the last time a mere thought nudged the compass of your life toward the extraordinary? Picture this: a world where each story opens doors you never knew existed. Imagine it. Now, let us embark on a journey through some tales of what could be, each a beacon in the fog of the everyday. But beware, for once you begin, you might find yourself...

I was enchanted by the possibilities that lay nestled in the crevices of your imagination.

With every heartbeat, the human spirit yearns for a glimpse of what could be, for the wisp of a dream that flutters just beyond the reach of reality. We are, by nature, creatures of boundless curiosity and relentless aspiration. Yet, in the hustle of the every day, the sparkle of our dreams often dims under the soot of the mundane. But what if I told you that within you lies an untapped wellspring of potential, a place where the seeds of positivity, once sown, could flourish into gardens of joy?

This is the astonishing truth: the narratives we tell ourselves shape the world we experience. Our thoughts, those ephemeral wisps that dance through the neural pathways of our brains, possess the power to carve canyons of change in the landscapes of our lives. This book, "Imagine," is a testament to that power. It is a collection of short stories, each beginning with a word that serves as both a command and an invitation: imagine.

The significance of this cannot be overstated. In a world that often feels bereft of hope, where headlines scream disaster and hearts grow weary with worry, the act of positive imagination is an act of rebellion. It is a declaration that we are not merely victims of circumstance but architects of our destiny. These stories emerge as lanterns in the darkness, guiding you through the mists of uncertainty to a place where the possible reigns supreme.

As you step into the unseen depths of this book, you will encounter visions of harmony, vignettes of triumph, and echoes of laughter that resonate with the rhythm of possibility. You will meet characters who, just like you, stand on the precipice of creation, their hearts ablaze with the promise of what might be. You will walk with them, hand in hand, as they step into worlds woven from the fabric of their aspirations.

But these are not mere flights of fancy. Each story is a mirror, a reflection that provokes thought and beckons you to ask the questions that linger in the corners of your consciousness. What if? Why not? How could this be? These questions are the keys to unlocking the doors of perception, swinging wide the gates to realms where positivity is the currency and hope.

As we bridge to discovery, you will find that these stories are more than mere words on a page. They are incantations, spells that, when spoken aloud, have the power to summon the most potent magic: the mind's magic. As you read, you will realize that you are not simply absorbing tales; you are creating, painting the canvas of your psyche with strokes of optimism and hues of potential.

Dare to imagine a world where each morning greets you with a symphony of potential. Envision a life where every challenge is a chrysalis, within which the butterfly of opportunity waits to emerge. Contemplate a reality where each act of kindness ripples through the cosmos, an eternal testament to the power of compassion.

Can you see it? Close your eyes for a moment and let the power of imagination sweep you away. Open them and see the world anew through the lens of what could be. With this vision, I, as a writer, invite you to join me on a journey of discovery and transformation. Within these pages, you will not merely read; embark upon an odyssey of the soul, a voyage that will chart a course to the shores of your most cherished dreams.

Let us begin with a simple word that is both the key to this collection and the doorway to infinite worlds: *Imagine.*

The Canvas of Life

Imagine Choosing Passion Over Pay Cheque

Imagine standing at the crossroads of life where each path is paved with the promise of future paycheque or the allure of passions pursued. Which path would you choose? This question, though simple, cuts to the very core of our existence, demanding introspection and honesty.

In the grand tapestry of modern society, woven with threads of ambition and success, we often find ourselves chasing after the security that comes with a hefty paycheque. But at what cost? Is the comfort of financial stability worth the price of a passion unfulfilled, a dream deferred?

Consider for a moment the world we inhabit—a world rife with individuals who trudge through their days; shoulders weighed down by the burden of unrequited aspirations. This is the central issue that we, as a collective, face: the sacrifice of our innermost yearnings on the altar of economic necessity.

It is no secret that most choose the conventional path, where the heart's desires are silenced by the clinking coins of practicality. From a young age, we are taught to aspire to careers that promise stability and prestige, often at the expense of our creative impulses or humanitarian leanings.

But what if we dared to defy this norm? What if the real solution to a life of fulfilment lies not in pursuing wealth but in passion? Imagine a world where vocations are chosen not by the size of the paycheck they promise but by the joy and satisfaction they bring.

As I reflect upon my journey from Iran's cultural crossroads to London's entrepreneurial avenues, I cannot help but recognize the transformative power of passion. It was not the allure of material riches that propelled me forward but the burning desire to make a meaningful impact, to weave a narrative of change and positivity through business, philanthropy and art.

This is not merely a call to abandon all practical concerns in favour of whimsical pursuits. Rather, it is an invitation to integrate your deepest passions into your professional life, to find a balance where your work becomes an extension of your very essence.

The implications of such a shift are profound, not just for the individual but for society as a whole. Engaging with our work on an emotional level can lead to a surge of creativity and innovation, as each person brings their unique perspective and enthusiasm to their field.

Imagine the masterpieces that could be created, the social issues that could be tackled with enthusiasm, and the technological advancements that could be pioneered—all because individuals chose to harness their intrinsic interests and talents.

And this connection to our work is not just about personal satisfaction; it's about creating a legacy that resonates with who we are at our core. It's about building a life that we can look back on, not regret or what-ifs, but with the pride of knowing we have lived true to ourselves.

To engage emotionally with this concept, envision yourself waking up each day with a fire in your belly, eager to face the challenges and triumphs of a career that aligns with your deepest passions. Picture the joy, the sense of purpose that could infuse every aspect of your life.

This is not a fairy tale or an unattainable dream. It is a choice, a deliberate decision to value the richness of experience over the richness of our bank accounts. It is the understanding that the accurate measure of wealth lies not in our financial assets but in our happiness and sense of fulfilment.

The path of passion is fraught with risks and uncertainties, yes. But it is also the path leading to the most beautiful destinations—destinations crafted from the very essence of who we are.

So, I ask you to imagine. Imagine the life you could lead, the impact you could have, and the satisfaction you could savour if you prioritize passion over paycheck. Imagine the world if we all took that leap of faith.

We stand on the brink of possibility. The question now is not whether we can afford to follow our passions but whether we can afford not to. Let us live not by the constraints of convention but by the beat of our hearts. Let us choose passion. Let us imagine.

Imagine Every Risk Taken Leads to Reward

A silent revolution brews in a landscape where ambition and security often lock horns. Picture a society where every gamble, every leap into the unknown, ends not in the crushing embrace of failure but in the exhilarating arms of success. This is the world I invite you to consider—a reality where each calculated risk is met with a tangible, positive outcome, forming the foundation of a culture steeped in innovation and boldness.

Now, cast your eyes upon the significant issue that shackles our collective potential: the fear of failure. A spectre haunts our minds' corridors, whispering cautions and conjuring images of disaster and ruin. The trepidation it instils is palpable, for the stakes in our current reality are high. Missteps can lead to financial ruin, social ostracism, or worse, the death of dreams.

If left unchecked, the consequences of this fear could be dire. A society paralyzed by the dread of taking chances is a society that stagnates. Without the willingness to venture beyond the familiar, progress is stifled, and innovation is smothered in its cradle. The cost is not only in the inventions unwrought and artworks uncreated but in the vibrancy of life itself.

But what if the solution lies in reprogramming our perception of risk and reward? What if we could cultivate an environment where each endeavour, each venture into the untested waters, was guaranteed to yield fruit?

Let's chart the course for such a solution. It begins with education—reshaping the narratives we tell our children and ourselves about success and failure. We must instil a new doctrine: that risk is not the enemy but a vital ally. By fostering a mindset that views potential losses as stepping stones rather than pitfalls, we can transform the very fabric of our decision-making processes.

Implementation of this bold new philosophy requires a multi-pronged approach. It calls for restructuring our educational systems to prioritize critical thinking and resilience. It demands an overhaul of our professional environments to encourage experimentation and forgive the inevitable misfires accompanying innovation. It needs a social support system that nurtures and celebrates the audacious ones who dare to dream.

Evidence of such strategies' effectiveness can be seen in the handful of organizations and societies that have embraced similar models. Look to the tech giants of Silicon Valley, where the mantra 'fail fast, fail often' underpins a culture of relentless advancement and unprecedented technological growth. Or consider the tiny Nordic countries, where social safety nets ensure entrepreneurs can take business risks without fearing destitution.

What if, however, this is not the only path? Alternatives do exist. One such is the fostering of strategic partnerships to mitigate individual risk. Another is using simulations and predictive modelling to gauge the potential outcomes of risk better before it is taken.

These words are not merely a fanciful flight of imagination. They are a clarion call to action—a summons to challenge the status quo and embrace a future where fear does not dictate our choices.

Can you envision a day when our headlines sing not about economic downturns but the boundless success stories of those who dared to dream? Imagine the art that might adorn our cities, the medical breakthroughs that could save lives, and the technological wonders that might redefine our existence.

Imagine a world where every risk led not to the quagmire of regret but to the exhilarating pinnacle of reward. It's a bold vision but one within our grasp. The question now is not of possibility but of will.

Do we possess the collective courage to reconstruct our reality? To cast aside the chains of trepidation and stride forward into a future where every risk is met with its due reward?

The pages ahead will not just muse upon this question; they will offer a blueprint for its realization. For in the heart of every risk lies the seed of reward, waiting for the brave to nurture it. It is time to take the gamble, embrace the unknown, and imagine that every risk taken leads to a reward.

Let us begin.

Imagine a Day of Universal Kindness

The dawn crept over the horizon with a tender glow, spilling light onto a world on the brink of transformation. It was a day like no other, not marked by the clamour of alarms or the grumble of traffic but by the harmonious melodies of birds and the soft whisper of trees swaying in the gentle breeze. The stage was set in a quaint town where the architecture was a tapestry of history and modernity, where the echoes of the past met the whispers of the future.

In this microcosm of society, the leading players were not the powerful or the privileged but the ordinary citizens: the baker, whose hands shaped dough with as much care as he shaped his children's morals; the teacher, whose lessons extended beyond the classroom; the elderly widow, whose stories of yesteryear were laced with wisdom; and the young entrepreneur, whose ambitions were tethered to the community's wellbeing. Each, in their own right, was an unwitting pioneer of what was to unfold.

The challenge was as old as time—indifference. A society that had, over generations, built invisible walls between hearts, where courtesy was often an afterthought and compassion a rare currency. But on this day, an unspoken pact was forged, as if the collective consciousness had reached a silent agreement to embrace pure kindness.

The approach was disarmingly simple yet revolutionary. Small acts multiplied exponentially—a greeting shared between strangers, a meal bought for the homeless man who had become part of the urban landscape, a listening ear offered to a friend in need. Though not coordinated, strategies of kindness seemed to ripple through the town with the synchronicity of a meticulously rehearsed ballet.

As if by magic, the results were immediate and palpable. Smiles became the day's motif, genuine and infectious. Once a canvas of solitude, the local park blossomed into a vibrant tapestry of community. Crime, often a byproduct of unaddressed pain, dwindled as empathy took its place. Economic transactions transformed into exchanges with goodwill, and productivity soared as people worked with joy rather than obligation.

Analyses and reflections on this phenomenon would later reveal profound insights. Productivity, it was found, didn't just rise; it transcended as individuals became invested in the collective success of their endeavours. Mental health statistics improved, with loneliness and depression receding like the tide. The town had become a case study, a microcosm that researchers would scrutinize, hoping to replicate its success on a larger scale.

Illustrations of the day's events were not confined to graphs and charts but captured in the heartfelt snapshots of shared laughter and communal effort. More than any data set, these images captured the essence of what had transpired.

The narrative of this extraordinary day connected to a larger concept—that kindness was not merely an act but a culture, a currency that could transform economies and societies. It was a powerful reminder that the most profound revolutions begin in the human heart.

As the sky turned to dusk and the stars blinked into existence, a question hung in the air, unspoken yet resonant: "What if every day could be like today?" It was an invitation to the reader, to the world, to continue the legacy of this single day of universal kindness.

I, Reza Abelechian, a wanderer of nations and a student of humanity, have laid before you a tapestry of possibilities. Born in the cradle of ancient civilization, nurtured in the progressive heart of Europe, and now a sojourner in the bustling metropolis of London, I have seen firsthand what the power of kindness can achieve.

The pages of this book are not merely filled with words but with a vision—a vision of a society reborn through the simple yet transformative act of kindness. As a businessman, I've seen kindness unlock potential and foster alliances. As a philanthropist, I've witnessed its power to heal and build bridges across divides.

So, I leave you with this final musing: Imagine a day when kindness is the norm, not the exception. Imagine a society where each individual acts with a heart unguarded, a world transformed by the purest form of connection. It begins with a simple act, a moment of empathy, a gesture of understanding. It starts with you.

Let us dare to imagine—and then create—a world where kindness reigns supreme.

Imagine Erasing 'What Ifs' From Your Vocabulary

The very essence of life is interwoven with the dreams we dare to dream and the choices we dare to make. From the recesses of our deepest desires, we conjure the strength to chase the shadows of doubt and cast light upon the paths we choose to tread. Imagine, if you will, a life unbridled by the chains of regret, a life where every 'what if' has been erased from the lexicon of our existence.

To navigate this thought, we must first acquaint ourselves with the terms that form the bedrock of our exploration. These terms are 'Regret,' 'Opportunity,' 'Choice,' and 'Growth'. Each word is a tile in the mosaic of understanding we are about to piece together.

'Regret' is the sorrow or remorse we feel when we reflect on past actions or inactions and wish we had done things differently. The shadow follows us, whispering of alternative outcomes that might have been. 'Opportunity,' its counterpart, is the set of circumstances that makes it possible to do something. It is the open door, the fork in the road, the blank canvas awaiting the first stroke of brilliance. 'Choice' is the act of selecting between two or more possibilities. It is the moment of truth, the crossroads where we assert our agency and steer our destiny. Lastly, 'Growth' is the process of developing or maturing physically, mentally, or spiritually. It is the fruit of our labours, the evidence of our journey, the tapestry woven from our experiences.

These terms are not merely academic; they are the essence of a life lived intentionally. When we understand 'regret,' we can learn to release its grip on our hearts. By recognizing 'opportunity,' we can become adept at seizing it with both hands. Understanding 'choice' empowers us to decide our paths with confidence. And 'growth' is the natural consequence of these actions, a testament to our resilience and capacity to evolve.

Consider, for a fleeting moment, the serendipity of a chance encounter that leads to a lifelong friendship or the split-second decision to take a different route home that opens the door to a new career path. These are not merely plot points in a grand narrative but real-world manifestations of our key terms. They are poignant, tangible examples of how life can flourish when we step beyond the shadows of hesitation and embrace the light of possibility.

Yet, as we turn the pages of this tome, we must resist the urge to summarize or conclude. There is no final chapter to this story, no neatly tied ribbon to signal its completion. Instead, there is an ongoing dialogue, a continuous exchange between the reader and the world around them.

The narrative of 'Imagine' is a tapestry woven from the threads of human experience, each strand a story, a lesson, a triumph. It is a call to arms, not of the violent kind, but a summoning of courage, the kind that propels us forward, undeterred by the fear of failure or the spectre of regret.

In the quiet moments, when the hum of the city recedes into the background and the weight of the day's choices rests heavily upon our shoulders, we may ask, "What if I had chosen differently?" But the beauty of this existence, the crux of the matter, is that we are granted a new canvas, a fresh opportunity to paint our masterpiece every day.

So, let us take up the brush, dip it into the vibrant colours of our dreams, and erase the 'what ifs' from our vocabulary with bold strokes. In their place, we will find the resounding affirmation of 'what is,' the symphony of a life lived without regret and the crescendo of seizing every opportunity. The dance of life awaits, and with each step, we grow, thrive, and become the authors of our own stories.

Imagine how boundless life can be when we replace the hesitation of 'what if' with the conviction of 'what will be.'

Imagine Life as a Masterpiece in Progress

In the grand gallery of existence, every soul is both an artist and a canvas, each day a brush stroke across the fabric of time. Envision life as the ultimate work of art, a masterpiece continually unfolding, each experience contributing to its depth and beauty. But what if we delve deeper into this analogy, teasing out the intricate threads that bind the notions of life and art together?

Contemplate for a moment the silent dialogue between the painter and the painting. With every colour chosen and a line drawn, the artist reveals their innermost emotions, thoughts, and spirit. Life, in its immeasurable complexity, mirrors this act of creation. Each decision we make, from the mundane to the monumental, is a reflection of our inner self, an indelible mark upon the canvas of our existence.

Why draw this parallel between life and art? It is to illuminate the profound truth that we are the creators of our reality. Through this lens, we may glean insights into the nature of our being and the fabric of our world. By establishing criteria such as intention, expression, and evolution, we can embark on a balanced comparison between the act of creating art and the act of living.

Consider intention in both realms. The artist approaches the canvas with a purpose, whether to capture a landscape bathed in the golden light of dusk or to convey the tumult of an emotional tempest. Similarly, we approach the moments of our lives with intentions, some as clear as the desire to achieve a specific goal, others as abstract as the pursuit of happiness.

Expression, too, serves as a poignant criterion. In art, it is the manifestation of vision and emotion, the brush strokes that bring a painting to life. In our lives, expression finds form in our words, our actions, and even our silence. Each is a deliberate choice, a component of the image we present to the world.

And what of evolution? The masterpiece that culminates an artist's career is often vastly different from their early works. It reflects growth in skill and perspective. So, does our life evolve, shaped by experiences, learning, and personal development?

Now, let us draw direct comparisons. The way a palette of colours can blend seamlessly or contrast sharply mirrors the harmony and discord we encounter in our relationships and endeavours. The bold lines and soft edges found in a painting are akin to the definitive decisions and gentle nudges we experience as we navigate life's complexities.

Yet, just as art and life run parallel, they also diverge. No two artists will interpret a scene similarly, just as no two individuals will live identical lives. The contrasts are as telling as the similarities. While art is often a solitary pursuit, life is undeniably a collective experience. The artist can start anew if the painting fails to satisfy, but we cannot erase the past; we must integrate every experience into the narrative of our lives.

Visual aids, though not applicable in the textual form, find their counterpart in the vivid imagery that language can evoke. Imagine the brush strokes as days spent under the vast expanse of sky, the colours as the emotions that play across our hearts, and the canvas as the world upon which we leave our mark.

As we delve into this analysis, insights emerge. The comparison reveals that life, like art, is never static. Each is subject to interpretation, change, to growth. The broader implications are clear: we possess the power to shape our lives with the same deliberation an artist employs to create a work of art.

We find a call to action in considering the real-world relevance of these theoretical musings. Just as the artist must continue to learn, experiment, and create, so must we persist in our pursuit of growth, meaning, and joy.

Gaze upon your life as the artist regards their canvas: with passion, intention, and the understanding that each moment is an opportunity to add depth and beauty to your masterpiece in progress. Let the past be the underpainting, essential but not final, and the future the layers yet to be applied, full of potential and promise.

Ask yourself, what hues will you choose for the dawn of tomorrow? What scenes will you paint upon the tapestry of your days? Will you stand before life's easel with trepidation or with the courage of an artist who knows that within them lies the power to create something truly magnificent?

Embrace the rhythm of your existence and the cadence of your experiences, and let them flow into the masterpiece you are crafting. And remember, profound beauty can be found in the simplicity of a single brush stroke or a single choice.

And so, with each day, with each decision, with the very beat of your heart, you are painting your life. A masterpiece in progress, a work of art that is uniquely and undeniably yours.

Harmony in Diversity

Imagine a World Without Borders

Imagine, just for a moment, that you hold in your hands not merely a book but a key to unlock a vision of the world as it could be, unshackled by the arbitrary lines that have divided humanity for centuries. This is not a fleeting daydream; it is the first step on a journey towards a reality where our shared humanity outshines the barriers of nationality.

As you delve deeper into these pages, you will encounter the scaffolding of a world built on the foundation of unity and understanding. I will share with you the insights gleaned from my life—a tapestry woven from the threads of diverse cultures, from the vibrant bazaars of Tehran to the tranquil shores of Denmark and the bustling heart of London. My experiences as a businessman and philanthropist have revealed to me the untapped potential in our collective synergy, and it is this revelation that I will unfold before you.

Perhaps you are sceptical. "A world without borders?" you might question. "Is it not a utopian fantasy?" Let me address your doubts head-on. The concept may seem daunting, even outlandish, but I assure you, the seeds of this transformation are already germinating. In this book, I will present real-world examples, innovative ideas, and social technologies bridging divides and fostering a global community. The change is not only possible—it is already in motion.

Now, I invite you to close your eyes for a brief interlude. Envision the human tapestry without the seams of borders, a society where the exchange of culture, ideas, and affection flows as freely as the wind across the plains. Imagine a child born into a world where the latitude and longitude of their birthplace do not predetermine their destiny. This is the metamorphosis that awaits us.

By committing to this exploration, you are not just reading but embarking on a transformative journey. The wisdom in these chapters can alter your perception, challenge the status quo, and inspire action. Together, we can redefine the meaning of community and citizenship globally.

Let us dive into the heart of the matter. What does a world without borders look like? Picture vibrant cities where multiculturalism isn't just accepted but celebrated, where the fusion of cuisines, languages, and traditions creates a mosaic richer than any singular culture could offer. Think of the economic prosperity that could be achieved when unrestricted collaboration and innovation are the norm, not the exception.

But how do we navigate the complexities of such a world? Here, the questions arise as naturally as the sun at dawn. How would we tackle the intricacies of law, the challenges of governance, or the protection of human rights? We shall tackle these questions not with vague notions but with concrete strategies and examples that demonstrate the art of the possible.

Consider the advancements in technology that have already made our world smaller. We can communicate instantaneously across continents, share knowledge at the click of a button, and build communities without regard to geography. Our economic systems are increasingly interdependent, a testament to the fact that cooperation can lead to greater prosperity than isolation ever could.

And yet, we mustn't forget the human element. For it is the stories of individuals, the faces of those who have crossed borders in search of a better life, and the hands of those who have extended beyond their reach to help another that will genuinely illustrate the beauty of our shared humanity.

These narratives will serve as the guiding stars on our voyage.

In the spirit of transparency, let me be clear: this transition will not be devoid of challenges. But as someone who has navigated the waters of change, I can attest to the resilience and adaptability of the human spirit. Every chapter of this book will reinforce your understanding and commitment to this vision, ensuring that when you turn the final page, you are not just a passive reader but an active participant in the genesis of a new world.

The time for idle speculation has passed. The moment has come to embrace the bold, the imaginative, the seemingly impossible. A world without borders is not just a fantasy— it is a destination. The path we carve together through these pages will lead us there, step by steadfast.

Let us embark on this journey not with trepidation but with the courage of conviction, the strength of unity, and the unyielding belief in our common destiny. Welcome to "Imagine a World Without Borders." Welcome to the dawn of a new era.

Imagine Every Language Spoken in One Song

In the grand tapestry of human history, few things have served as a more potent symbol of unity and understanding than music. It transcends language, culture, and time barriers, offering a common thread by which all can connect. But what if we could expand that connection, weaving every tongue spoken across the globe into a harmonious melody? This is the vision of "Imagine Every Language Spoken in One Song," a story that chronicles the history of language and the unifying power of music as a universal language.

From the dawn of communication, when our ancestors first carved symbols onto cave walls or sent smoke signals rippling into the sky, the need to connect, share, and belong has been an immutable part of the human condition. The origins of language are shrouded in time's mist, but scholars agree that the earliest forms of structured communication likely emerged alongside the early human communities in Africa. As these communities grew and spread across the earth, so did the diversity of languages, each a unique prism to understand the world.

Tracing the odyssey of language, one encounters the Rosetta Stone, an ancient slab that cracked open the secrets of Egyptian hieroglyphs. Fast forward through time and witness the printing press' invention, catapulting language and culture dissemination. These milestones marked a technological leap and a profound shift in how humans connected and communicated.

Imagine now the cascading notes of a song as they leap from the page, each one a word from a different tongue. Could visual aids convey the complex symphony of a global language? Perhaps a diagram could represent the network of linguistic roots, branches spreading out to touch every corner of the earth, or an image capturing the moment when voices from across the world rise in a single song.

Within this grand chorus, the cultural and regional variations are not lost but celebrated. The linguistic diversity from the indigenous tribes of the Amazon rainforest to the bustling cities of Asia is not a barrier but a source of richness. How language has evolved across cultures reflects humanity—varied, complex, and beautiful.

In the modern era, interpretations of language and music have taken new forms. Technology has given rise to virtual choirs, where voices from across the globe are stitched together into a seamless performance, defying physical boundaries. Social media platforms broadcast the polyphonic texture of world languages, making it possible for a song to be sung in a multiplicity of tongues yet united in its melody and meaning.

But this journey is not without its challenges. Linguists lament the extinction of languages at an alarming rate, with a language dying approximately every two weeks. Each lost language is a verse silenced in the song of humanity. Controversies also arise over the homogenization of culture, with global languages overshadowing smaller tongues. Yet, in these turning points lies opportunity— initiatives to preserve endangered languages are gaining traction, and artists are increasingly incorporating diverse languages into their work, reflecting the mosaic of human expression.

Have you ever wondered what speaking a language other than your own means? Learning another's tongue unlocks a door to their world and understanding the cadence of their thoughts and the poetry of their soul. It's a powerful bridge to empathy and solidarity.

Across the vast expanse of history, languages have risen and fallen, but music has endured. The rhythm of a drumbeat, the strum of a lyre, the hum of a mother's lullaby—all are threads in the fabric of our shared existence.

Let's pause for a moment and consider this: What if the next time you heard a song, you weren't just moved by the melody and the profound unity of the voices in multilingual verse?

The concept of a song blending every language is not merely a symbolic gesture but a call to action, a reminder that despite our many tongues, we share one voice—one humanity. It's an invitation to set aside differences and to celebrate the diversity that contributes to the richness of our collective experience.

As we move forward, we must ask ourselves how to contribute to this chorus. How can we ensure that no voice is left out, that every language finds its note in the symphony of human connection? It is not just a narrative; it's a living, breathing movement. It's a commitment to unity in diversity, to understanding beyond words. It is an unfolding story, and with each word you read, you become a part of it. So, let us raise our voices together, and may the song we create resonate for generations to come.

Imagine Cultures Celebrating Each Other

In the intricate dance of humanity, myriad cultures whirl, each moving to the rhythm of its drumbeat, yet all part of a grander ballet that speaks to a shared existence. It is a world rich with the vibrant hues of tradition, the textures of history, and the melodies of myriad languages that echo the diversity of the human spirit. This narrative seeks not merely to observe this dance from afar but to step into the circle, join hands, and celebrate the manifold ways in which cultures enrich our global society.

Imagine, if you will, a world where the beauty of difference is not merely tolerated but exalted, where traditions from across the globe are recognized for their unique splendour to the tapestry of human experience. This celebration of cultural diversity is akin to an everlasting festival, where each culture showcases its heritage with pride and receives admiration in return.

At the heart of this vision lies a compelling proposition: cultural exchange is key to fostering a more harmonious and understanding world. It is not enough to simply coexist; we must actively embrace and uplift one another's cultural legacies, learning from them and allowing our perspectives to be broadened and enriched in the process.

To bolster this claim, we turn to the concrete evidence found in the annals of history and the contemporary stage of global interaction. Consider the Silk Road, that ancient network of trade routes that facilitated the exchange of goods and acted as a conduit for cultural exchange between the East and West. Through these interactions, art, religion, technology, and cuisine were shared and transformed, leaving an indelible imprint on the societies they touched.

Delving further into this evidence, we uncover stories of travellers like Ibn Battuta and Marco Polo, whose journeys exemplified the richness of cultural exchange. They traversed vast distances and brought back with them tales and knowledge that sparked their contemporaries' imaginations and continue to captivate us today.

Yet, in presenting this case for the celebration of cultures, one must also acknowledge the counterarguments. Some fear that cultural exchange can lead to the dilution or loss of traditions and that the dominant cultures may overshadow the lesser known. This is a valid concern, and history does provide examples of cultural assimilation that have led to the erosion of indigenous customs and languages.

In response, it is crucial to differentiate between cultural exchange that is reciprocal and respectful and that which is imposed and assimilative. A true celebration of cultures involves mutual sharing and an equal platform for expression. It is about creating spaces where all cultures can thrive and be appreciated for their unique contributions.

Further supporting evidence of the benefits of cultural celebration comes from the realm of festivals and international events. Festivals such as Diwali, Carnival, and the Chinese New Year have transcended their original cultural boundaries and are now enjoyed by people of diverse backgrounds around the world. These events serve as opportunities for cultural immersion and understanding, breaking down barriers and nurturing a sense of global community.

In conclusion, as we draw the threads of this narrative together, the assertion that cultural exchange is beneficial and essential to the human experience is reinforced. It is a clarion call to recognize and celebrate the myriad traditions that make up the mosaic of humanity. Each culture's unique practices, stories, and wisdom add depth and richness to the collective human journey. They are not mere relics of the past to be observed in museums but living, breathing customs to be experienced, shared, and honoured.

As we look to the future, let us aspire to foster a world where every cultural expression is valued and where learning from one another is a source of joy and growth. Let us build bridges of understanding that span the chasms of ignorance and fear. Imagine a world where cultures celebrating each other is not an exception but the norm, where the symphony of humanity is played in a harmonious chorus of varied but united voices. This is the world we can create together, and it begins with the simple yet profound act of celebration.

Imagine Ethnicity Being a Cause for Celebration

In a world teeming with a kaleidoscope of ethnic identities, envision a society where each cultural thread is woven with respect and joy into the fabric of our shared tapestry. Picturing such a society is not merely a daydream; it is a feasible ambition, a summit that humanity can strive to reach with concerted effort and unwavering commitment. Through this journey, I will guide you along a path of transformative action, leading to a future where ethnicity becomes a cause for celebration, not conflict.

Establish the Goal:

Our collective aim is to cultivate a society where ethnic diversity is accepted and celebrated with genuine enthusiasm. This society will understand that every ethnic group, with its unique customs, languages, and worldviews, enriches the human experience. By the end of this roadmap, you will be equipped with the knowledge and strategies to contribute actively to this vibrant, inclusive world.

List the Necessary Materials or Prerequisites:

To achieve this vision, several prerequisites are essential. Foremost is an open heart and mind, ready to embrace and learn from the full spectrum of human diversity. Additionally, access to education that highlights the value of ethnic diversity and promotes intercultural competencies is paramount. Other key materials include platforms for interethnic dialogue, policies that protect cultural heritage, and media and leaders' commitment to represent all ethnicities equitably.

Begin with a Broad Overview:

The journey to celebrating ethnicity encompasses several phases: fostering awareness, building bridges, implementing inclusive policies, creating celebratory platforms, and continuously nurturing interethnic appreciation. Each phase builds upon the last, creating a robust structure for a society that thrives on its diversity.

Dive into Detailed Steps:

Firstly, fostering awareness involves education and exposure. Curricula from early childhood should include stories and histories from various ethnic backgrounds, promoting understanding from a young age. Media representation also plays a role; it must reflect diversity as an exception and the norm.

Building bridges requires intentional efforts to create spaces for interethnic dialogue and exchange. Community events, cultural fairs, and interethnic forums can serve as platforms where people learn from and about each other, fostering empathy and camaraderie.

Implementing inclusive policies ensures that all ethnic groups have equal opportunities and representation. This can involve reforming legal frameworks to protect against discrimination and to promote cultural preservation.

Creating celebratory platforms can take the form of festivals, holidays, and awards that recognize and honour the contributions of different ethnic groups. Such celebrations can transform respect and appreciation into a visible and tangible experience.

Continuously nurturing interethnic appreciation is an ongoing process. It involves regular reflection on our biases, a commitment to lifelong learning, and active participation in cultural exchanges.

Offer Tips and Warnings:

While engaging in this transformative work, remember that patience and persistence are virtues. Change may be gradual, but each step forward creates ripples. Be wary of tokenism or superficial acknowledgements of diversity; strive for meaningful engagement and deep respect.

Testing or Validation:

The success of this vision can be measured in the interactions between individuals of different ethnicities. Do respect and curiosity characterize them? Is there equitable representation in media, politics, and business? These are signs that society is moving in the right direction.

Troubleshooting (optional):

Challenges will arise, such as resistance to change or the entrenchment of stereotypes. In these instances, return to dialogue and education. Engage critics with empathy, and use setbacks to deepen your understanding and refine your approach.

Imagine a world where every encounter with someone from a different ethnicity adds a new hue to your understanding of humanity. Imagine a society where ethnic festivals are not just for those of a particular background but are embraced by all as opportunities for joyous participation and learning.

Can you see it? Can you feel the pulse of a society that dances to the rhythm of diversity, where every individual's ethnic heritage is a note in a grand symphony of human culture? It is not an unreachable star but a possible reality that begins with our collective imagination and is realized through our actions.

Let us then take up the challenge with the knowledge that our efforts to celebrate ethnicity can forge a future where every person's heritage is not a barrier but a bridge to greater understanding and unity. Together, let's turn the page to a new chapter in human history, where 'Imagine' becomes 'We did.'

Imagine Religions Bridging the Gap of Beliefs

In the intricate weave of human society, faith has often stood as a beacon of hope, a source of solace, and a guiding star. Yet, in the very same breath, it has erected walls of division, sown the seeds of discord, and ignited the flames of intolerance. Imagine a world where these disparate threads are entwined not to create boundaries but to bridge the vast expanse between hearts and souls. This is the essence of our narrative—a tale of convergence where the spiritual paths of many converge to create a sanctuary of shared wisdom and collective enlightenment.

The stage is set against the backdrop of a global tableau, where the clamour of discordant doctrines often drowns the symphony of shared human values. The challenge is not trivial; it is the herculean task of transcending entrenched dogmas to uncover a common spiritual ground.

The magnitude of this problem cannot be overstated. It has been the invisible architect of history's most persistent and painful schisms and the potent fuel for conflicts that have left deep scars on humanity's collective psyche. If left unaddressed, our path may lead us into the shadowy valleys of perpetual misunderstanding, where the light of compassion grows dim, and the possibility of a unified human family becomes a fading dream.

But what if we dared to imagine a solution? What if we envisioned a world where interfaith dialogues and ecumenical movements become the norm rather than the exception? A world where the wisdom of the Vedas, the compassion of the Buddha, the love preached by Christ, and the brotherhood espoused by Prophet Muhammad are seen as varied expressions of the same underlying truth?

The method to manifest this vision is rooted in the process of transformative engagement. It begins with dialogue—open, honest conversations where beliefs are shared, not to proselytize but to understand. It is a dialogue marked not by the compulsion to respond but by the willingness to listen.

To implement this vision, we must initiate forums at every level of society—from the local community to the global stage—where leaders and laypeople alike can engage in a spiritual exchange. Educational systems must be reformed to include the study of world religions, painting each faith with the brush of objectivity and respect.

Evidence of the effectiveness of interfaith dialogue is not merely anecdotal. Cities that have embraced such initiatives report lower levels of communal violence and higher rates of societal harmony. Studies also suggest that individuals involved in interfaith activities demonstrate more empathy and are likelier to engage in social action that transcends religious boundaries.

Yet, there are alternative paths to consider. Some advocate for a secular approach, where religion is entirely removed from the public sphere. Others propose a syncretic model, amalgamating various beliefs into a new, singular faith. While these ideas merit discussion, they often overlook the profound personal connection many feel to their religious identity.

Aren't there moments when we question the very foundation of our beliefs? What if the answer lies not in the erasure of these identities but in their celebration within a framework of mutual respect and universal values?

Let us distil our message to its essence to eschew superfluous adjectives and adverbs. This is a call to action for the architects of the future and the guardians of the present. It is a call to build bridges where moats have been dug to light lamps in the darkest of divides.

And so, we return to the rhythm of the human heart, the cadence of shared aspirations. Imagine a world where the call to prayer mingles with the ringing of church bells, where a kirtan's chant harmonizes with the Torah's recitation. If only we extend our hands to embrace unity; it is a world within our grasp.

In the silent spaces between our words, let us find the courage to ask ourselves: Can we afford not to try? Can we ignore the profound potential of a unified spiritual human community? The answer, whispered on the winds of change, resounds with a hopeful affirmation.

Imagine a sanctuary of faith, not bound by the rigid strictures of dogma but woven with the golden threads of shared human dignity. Here, on the pages of this vision, we find the blueprint for a future where religions bridge the gap of beliefs and 'Imagine' transforms into 'We are one.'

Sustainable Futures

Imagine Clean Energy Powering the World

In a vision as bright as the sun's rays, we embark on a journey toward a future where clean energy is the beating heart of our planet's life force. This is a world where the air is as pure as the intentions behind each watt of power generated, the seas are as calm as the steady hum of wind turbines, and the earth thrives, unburdened by the weight of carbon footprints. As we step into this chapter, we sketch out the blueprint for a utopia powered by the whispers of wind, the dance of sunlight, and the strength of water.

Our mission is unmistakable: to transition our global society to one powered entirely by renewable energy sources. This is the path to healing our world, ensuring the well-being of all its inhabitants, and crafting a legacy that future generations will speak of with gratitude.

The prerequisites are as vast as they are vital to achieving this monumental goal. We need technological innovation, political will, economic investment, and a cultural shift toward sustainability. From individual homeowners installing solar panels to governments enacting policies favouring renewable energy, every action contributes to the mosaic of change.

The roadmap to a clean energy future comprises several key milestones: the expansion of renewable energy sources, the modernization of energy infrastructure, the electrification of transportation, and the cultivation of energy efficiency. Each milestone is a stepping stone that carries us closer to our destination.

Firstly, we expand renewable energy sources, scaling up the production of solar, wind, hydroelectric, tidal, geothermal, and biomass energies. Each source requires a tailored approach—solar farms sprawling across deserts, offshore wind farms rising like forests in the sea, and hydroelectric plants harnessing the relentless flow of our rivers.

With the energy sources set, we turn to modernizing our infrastructure. Smart grids that communicate and respond to energy demands, energy storage systems that capture the power of the sun even when it sets, and transmission lines that deliver clean electricity across continents are all integral components of this modernization.

The transportation sector is revolutionizing as we electrify everything from commuter cars to long-haul trucks. Charging stations become as commonplace as streetlights, and innovations in battery technology make clean vehicles more efficient and accessible than ever before.

Finally, energy efficiency has become the silent hero of the clean energy era. Buildings are designed or retrofitted to sip rather than gulp energy, appliances operate precisely to minimize waste, and individuals adopt lifestyle changes that reduce their energy footprint.

As we navigate this transition, remember that the road is long and the work is hard, but the rewards are immeasurable. Invest in quality when choosing renewable technologies, and beware of false economies. Efficiency is your ally—embrace it in every aspect of life. And always look to the horizon, but don't overlook the power of local action.

Success in our endeavours is measured not just in gigawatts but in the air we breathe, our climate's stability, and our communities' health. We validate our progress through decreased emissions, increased biodiversity, and a thriving green economy.

Challenges will arise, be they technological obstacles or political resistance. When faced with such hurdles, return to the core principles of innovation, collaboration, and perseverance. Seek sustainable and equitable solutions, and rally the community around the shared vision of a cleaner, brighter future.

Can you picture it? The world we're striving toward? It's a canvas of opportunity, painted with the broad strokes of ambition and the fine lines of meticulous planning.

Something is intoxicating about the thought of a planet in harmony with its energy needs. The rustle of leaves in a forest no longer threatened by acid rain, the laughter of children in cities where the sky is no longer a canvas of smog, the quiet pride of a community that powers itself—these are the snapshots of a world running on clean energy.

In one bold statement, let it be said: this is our chosen future. Not because it is easy but because we cannot—must not—shirk the responsibility to the earth that cradles us and to the children who inherit it.

In the words of pioneers past, we have only just begun to tap into the vast potential of our planet's generosity. As the day closes and the first stars twinkle to life in the evening sky, let us make a silent vow to ourselves and the earth: we will tread lightly, we will power wisely, and we will imagine a world where clean energy is the only energy that lights up the night.

Imagine Oceans Teeming With Life

As the echoes of past ambitions for a world powered by the whispers of wind and the dance of sunlight settle in our minds, let us turn our attention to the vast, blue expanses that embrace our continents—the oceans. These waters, which have cradled life since time immemorial, have witnessed the ebb and flow of history's tide, shaping the destiny of our blue planet.

Travel back to the Industrial Revolution, a pivotal moment when human ingenuity sparked a blazing trail of progress. This era saw a surge in technological advancements but also began a relentless assault on marine environments. Factories belched pollutants, and ships began to crisscross the seas, leaving trails of oil and ballast water in their wake.

Historical milestones further sculpted our relationship with the oceans. The advent of commercial whaling brought giants to the brink of extinction, while the introduction of synthetic chemicals and plastics in the 20th century added insidious threats to marine life. As nations grew and economies expanded, the oceans became the ultimate sink for human waste, with devastating consequences.

From past to present, the tapestry of human progress is woven with threads of environmental impact. Today, we face the culmination of centuries of exploitation—oceans that are warmer, more acidic, and struggling to support the richness of life they once boasted. Coral reefs bleach into graveyards, fisheries collapse under the weight of overharvesting, and plastic gyres swirl like silent cyclones, entangling the innocent.

Why does history matter now? Understanding our past is akin to charting a course through treacherous waters. Only by recognizing the reefs of mistakes and the currents of consequences can we navigate toward a future where the oceans teem with life once more. The lessons of history are lanterns illuminating the path to restoration and balance.

And so, we segue to the story that unfolds beneath the waves. Imagine oceans brimming with life, a testament to the resilience of nature and the restorative touch of mindful stewardship. Picture the resurgence of coral reefs, vibrant and bustling with the activity of countless species, each playing their role in a harmonious symphony of marine life.

Can you see it? The water is clear, dancing with the shimmering light of a thousand suns, as fish of every hue dart among the crevices. The air is filled with the salty tang of a sea untainted by the toxins of yesteryear. This is not a dream but a vision—a vision we have the power to turn into reality.

Do you ever wonder how the whales might sing in a sea that is a sanctuary, not a battleground? Imagine their haunting melodies, no longer muffled by the drone of engines or the clang of industrial might but echoing pure and true from the abyss to the starlight.

In the grand narrative of the oceans, every creature has its verse. The humble krill, the majestic shark, the playful dolphin—each is a note in an aquatic symphony that has played since the dawn of time. Now, we must become the conductors of a revival, guiding each note back to its rightful place in the melody of the sea.

How do we begin this symphony of renewal? It starts with a single, resolute decision to respect and protect. From the smallest act of refusing a plastic straw to the global commitment to reducing carbon emissions, every choice weaves a thread of change into the future fabric.

Dive deep with me now into the heart of the ocean, where life abounds in forms too numerous to count. Here, in the silent depths, we find the resilience to inspire our journey.

The pressure is immense, the darkness complete, yet life thrives with an otherworldly beauty. If such wonders can exist here, what might we achieve in the sunlit waters above if we only dare to imagine?

Let this be our legacy: when faced with the choice between convenience and conservation, we choose the latter. We decided to be the caretakers of an ocean that does not choke on our refuse but breathes with the vibrancy of a world reborn.

In the words of those who have witnessed the ocean's depths and returned to tell the tale, the sea does not forgive or forget. It is time we extend the same courtesy, remembering the scars we have inflicted and forging a bond of healing in their stead.

As the day wanes and the horizon blurs into twilight, let us cast our sights on the promise of a dawn where the oceans are not mere witnesses to history but participants in a future written with the ink of sustainable choices.

Imagine oceans teeming with life, and know it is within our grasp to make it so. Let us take up this challenge with the vigour of the tides and the patience of the continents. For in the grand story of our planet, the chapter of life is still being written, and we hold the pen.

Imagine Cities as Hubs of Green Innovation

Imagine cities transformed into verdant utopias, where the concrete jungles of yesteryears have given way to a new era of ecological enlightenment. Envision urban landscapes not as they are but as they could be—vibrant mosaics of green innovation, where every rooftop, every street, and every breath of air is a testament to the harmony between human habitation and the natural world.

What if the sprawling metropolises that have long been the engines of progress became the cradles of a sustainability revolution? Could we dream of urban centres where green spaces and cutting-edge technologies flourish alongside one another, crafting a future that is as kind to the Earth as it is conducive to the bustling pace of city life?

With the dawn of this new chapter, we're faced with an unsettling truth: our cities, as they stand, are on a collision course with the environment. They are the pulsating heartbeats of civilization, yet they account for a staggering majority of carbon emissions and waste. The very foundations of our urban existence are riddled with inefficiencies, from energy consumption to transportation, and the repercussions of our actions cast a long, dark shadow over the prospects of future generations.

Picture the consequences if we maintain our current trajectory: a world where air quality plummets, water sources become tainted, and green spaces shrink into obscurity. Skies once blue are now shrouded in a perpetual haze, and its inhabitants' wheezing coughs drown out the city life's cacophony. This is a future no one wishes for—an urban dystopia where the chokehold of pollution stifles the promise of advancement.

But the pen is in our hands, and the page is unturned. The solutions lie before us, scattered like seeds waiting to take root. We need only the resolve to plant them.

One such seed is the green retrofitting of existing infrastructure. By infusing eco-friendly design into the very bones of our buildings, we can reduce energy consumption and create self-sustaining ecosystems within the cityscape. Solar panels could bask atop skyscrapers, wind turbines might whisper between them, and gardens could drape the walls like nature's tapestries.

What steps must we take to cultivate this green renaissance? It begins with policy, with incentives that encourage developers and homeowners alike to embrace the green revolution. It thrives through innovation, with research and technology paving the way for more innovative, efficient materials and construction methods. It requires a collective effort, a symphony of change-makers—engineers, architects, city planners, and citizens—all playing their part.

Some cities have already taken up the mantle, beacons of hope casting their light on the path ahead. For instance, Copenhagen's commitment to becoming carbon-neutral by 2025 is a bold declaration of intent. Green roofs, extensive bike lanes, and investments in renewable energy are but a few strokes of genius in their impressive repertoire.

But what of the alternatives to these green innovations? Some argue for a return to rural living to decentralize and reduce the strain on urban centres. Others advocate for technological solutions that may seem plucked from the pages of science fiction—like buildings that scrub carbon from the air or roads that charge electric cars as they drive.

Yet, these ideas are not mutually exclusive. A tapestry of solutions, woven together, might form the robust, resilient fabric we need to protect our urban environments. It's a matter of perspective, of daring to imagine and then acting with conviction.

So, let me ask you, dear reader: Can you envision a city where the rustling of leaves replaces the hum of traffic? Where is the skyline not merely a silhouette of steel and glass but a living, breathing organism that nurtures its inhabitants?

This is no mere fantasy; it's a blueprint for a sustainable future, a dream that demands to be realized. It's a narrative of hope, etched into the streets we walk upon, written in the wind that courses through our concrete and steel canyons.

The cities of tomorrow need not be the heavy hand that tips the balance of our fragile ecosystem. They can be the cradles of a new age, the forges of a future where innovation and nature intersect. It's a vision within reach— a world where our urban hearts beat not against nature but in unison with it.

Let us take that bold step forward into a realm where cities are not just habitable but hospitable to the world they inhabit. Imagine such a place, and then strive to make it so. Join me in this journey, where every brick laid and every tree planted is a verse in the epic of our time. Let us be the architects of a legacy that future generations will look upon, not with despair, but with gratitude.

The page awaits, and the pen is poised; let us write a story of renewal, of cities reborn as hubs of green innovation. Can you imagine?

Imagine Endangered Species Thriving Once Again

Nestled in the emerald embrace of the sprawling Amazon rainforest, a chorus of life heralds the dawn. Scarlet macaws, with their vibrant plumage, paint the sky with streaks of colour as they take flight among the treetops. Below, the forest floor teems with the stealthy movements of the jaguar, the silent whispers of their paws a testament to nature's cautious balance. This is a world reborn from the brink, a testament to the resilience of life and the power of concerted human effort.

I am Reza Abelechian, a man of varied lands and experiences. Born under the Iranian sun, raised amidst the Danish winds, and settled in London's ceaseless bustle, I've traversed diverse geographical and professional realms. As a businessman, I've seen the stark realities of commerce and its impact on our planet. As a philanthropist, I've sought to mend the tears in the fabric of our ecosystems. And as a writer, I now weave tales of hope—stories of a world where humanity and nature coexist in harmony.

But let us turn our gaze to the heart of this narrative, where the bold stripes of the Sumatran tiger once again roam freely through the dense underbrush of their Indonesian home. These majestic felines, symbols of untamed wilderness, faced the spectre of extinction. Their challenge? A dwindling habitat, poached for human greed and fragmented by the relentless march of deforestation.

The approach to their salvation was as multifaceted as the stripes on their backs. Conservationists collaborated globally, understanding that the plight of the Sumatran tiger was a puzzle requiring many hands. Sanctuaries were established, poaching laws were enforced with new vigour, and local communities were engaged as stewards of these jungles. Technology lent a hand—drones monitored vast expanses while genetic studies ensured the vitality of the tiger's bloodlines.

The results? A burgeoning population, cubs born into a world more welcoming than their ancestors. A 20% increase in their numbers over a decade, a figure that might seem modest but roars with significance. Each additional tiger is a stripe in the canvas of conservation success; each territory reclaimed a victory against the odds.

Reflection upon these outcomes yields a spectrum of emotions—pride in what has been achieved and caution for the path ahead. Criticism comes with the territory; some argue that the funds could serve needy humans. Yet, is it not a service to humanity to preserve the wonders of our planet? What are we, if not part of this intricate web of life?

Images of these creatures, captured by camera traps, serve as visual aids to our story. They are proof of life's tenacity and our capacity to correct the course of our narratives.

But the tale of the Sumatran tiger is a chapter in a grander tome of environmental reclamation. It connects to a larger narrative that speaks of balance and the interdependence of all species. It is a tale not of dominion but of cohabitation.

As you turn the pages of this unfolding story, consider the silent question that hovers like a butterfly over a meadow of wildflowers: What world do we wish to leave behind? Will future generations speak of the tiger, the macaw, and other creatures as legends lost to time? Or will they walk in a world where the roar of the tiger and the song of the macaw is but a natural part of the tapestry of life?

The power of imagination is not merely in constructing fantasy but in the blueprint it provides for reality. We have imagined cities as hubs of green innovation; now, let us imagine a world where no species are left behind and the endangered thrive again.

Take a moment to envision the earth beneath your feet—a soil rich with the possibility of rebirth. Look around you and see the world not for what it is but for what it could be. A canvas awaits, the colours of life ready to be brushed onto its expanse by hands, both human and divine.

Imagine such a world, and let that vision guide your steps. For in the imagining, we find the seeds of reality, and in planting those seeds, we find hope for all that breathes, crawls, and roams upon this shared planet of ours.

The story continues, and with it, our role as authors of destiny. Will you join me in this quest for renewal? Can you imagine?

Imagine Plastic-Free Nature Trails

Imagine stepping onto a trail where the crunch of leaves underfoot is the only sound that breaks the silence. Look around and witness the branches sway gently, the leaves rustling in a soft symphony with the wind. The air is crisp, filled with the earthy scent of moss and pine. It's a place where the only signs of human presence are the footprints left behind, not the discarded relics of consumption. This is the world we have shaped, a world where nature trails are pristine, untouched by the scourge of plastic waste, and every step taken is a step towards reconnecting with the earth.

As we delve into this narrative, consider the claim at its heart: removing plastic waste from our nature trails is a possibility and a reality achieved through concerted human effort. The evidence is tangible, found in the data collected from global cleanup initiatives, which reveal a significant reduction in plastic debris in these natural sanctuaries. Reports from environmental organizations show a decline in plastic pollution due to the ban on single-use plastics and the rise in eco-consciousness among travellers and hikers.

Take a closer look at these efforts. Volunteers gather, armed with gloves and bags, passion fueling their dedication as they comb through the underbrush, removing every piece of plastic in their path. Policies have changed, too, with stringent regulations on plastic packaging and the implementation of 'Leave No Trace' principles becoming commonplace. Companies have risen to the challenge, producing biodegradable alternatives to traditional snack wrappers and water bottles as hikers embrace the philosophy of carrying out what they carry.

Yet, some argue that the focus on plastic waste detracts from other pressing environmental issues, such as climate change or habitat destruction. They contend that resources could be better allocated and that perhaps the fight against plastic is a distraction from larger, more complex problems. However, a rebuttal lies in the interconnectedness of these issues. Reducing plastic waste is a cog in the wheel of broader environmental stewardship. By protecting our trails from plastic, we safeguard the habitats that support biodiversity, contribute to carbon sequestration, and foster a more profound respect for nature that transcends into other conservation areas.

Additional evidence supports this holistic view. Studies suggest that areas free from plastic pollution see a resurgence in native flora and fauna, which in turn attracts eco-tourism, bolstering local economies and promoting sustainable practices. The health of our trails reflects our planet's health; as such, every victory against plastic is a victory for the Earth.

In conclusion, the assertion that we can live in a world with plastic-free nature trails is not a fanciful dream but a reinforced reality. The trails we tread are the arteries of the Earth, and by keeping them free from plastic, we allow the lifeblood of nature to flow freely. We've witnessed the rebirth of ecosystems once choked by waste and seen the return of species once driven away by our carelessness. Our journey is not over; it's a path that requires constant vigilance and dedication. But as we move forward, let us carry the lessons learned and the successes earned, using them to fuel our continued commitment to a cleaner, greener, and more connected world.

Imagine a future where our children will know nothing of plastic-ridden trails, where they will learn of our past not as a cautionary tale but as a historical turning point. Envision a world where the beauty of nature is unmarred by human folly, where each step on a nature trail is a step into a legacy of preservation. Imagine, and then make it so. For in our imagination lies the blueprint for action and in our action, the hope for a thriving, vibrant planet.

Technological Utopias

Imagine AI as Humanity's Helping Hand

In the brisk dawn of a new era, we stand on the cusp of a revolution so profound it whispers of a renaissance, heralding a paradigm where artificial intelligence is not a distant behemoth of science fiction but a tactile, invaluable ally in our everyday lives. Imagine, if you will, a future where AI doesn't loom over humanity but extends a hand to lift it higher to realms of potential hitherto unexplored.

Artificial Intelligence, or AI, as it is colloquially termed, refers to the simulation of human intelligence in machines. These machines are designed to think like humans and mimic their actions. The term may also be applied to any machine that exhibits traits associated with a human mind, such as learning and problem-solving.

The key elements of AI include machine learning, where computers learn new things without being explicitly programmed; natural language processing, which allows machines to understand and respond to human language; and robotics, a branch of AI that involves designing and manufacturing robots that can do tasks that humans find difficult or dangerous.

Tracing its etymological roots, the term "artificial intelligence" was first coined in 1955 by John McCarthy, a computer scientist who organized the famous Dartmouth Conference in 1956. Here, AI was defined as a field, and its goals and objectives were laid out.

To contextualize AI within a broader framework, it serves as a cornerstone of the fourth industrial revolution, an era characterized by blurred lines between the physical, digital, and biological spheres. AI is the linchpin that holds these realms together, driving innovation and efficiency across industries.

Real-world applications of AI are diverse and transformative. AI algorithms can analyze medical images to detect diseases more accurately in healthcare than human radiologists. In finance, AI systems can manage investments, optimize stock portfolios, and see fraudulent transactions with a precision that dwarfs human capabilities. Virtual assistants like Siri and Alexa have become ubiquitous in everyday life, helping people manage their schedules, control smart home devices, and access information hands-free.

Despite its widespread adoption, AI is often encumbered with misconceptions. One common fallacy is the belief that AI can only lead to job displacement and unemployment. While it is true that AI can automate specific tasks, it also creates new job opportunities. It enhances human productivity by taking on mundane and repetitive tasks, allowing humans to focus on creative and strategic endeavours.

Envisage a world where AI catalyzes human creativity. Artists employ algorithmic companions to push the boundaries of music, painting, and literature. At the same time, scientists utilize AI to uncover the secrets of the cosmos, peering more profound into the fabric of reality than ever before. Even the most ordinary interactions are imbued with a layer of intelligence as AI personalizes and streamlines our experiences.

Why, then, do some view AI with trepidation? It is the unknown that often breeds fear. But with understanding comes acceptance, and with acceptance comes the opportunity to wield AI as a tool for the betterment of society.

Can you imagine a day without the seamless assistance of AI? Our reliance on this technology grows as it becomes more ingrained in our daily routines. The subtle recommendations on your streaming service, the dynamic brake system in your vehicle, the predictive text on your smartphone—all these conveniences are courtesy of AI's invisible hand.

A one-line paragraph for emphasis: AI is the unseen artisan of our digital age.

In crafting this future, we must use language that resonates with all, not just the technocrats. The power of AI should not be locked away behind walls of jargon and complexity. Instead, it should be shared, with simplicity being the key to unlocking its potential.

Consider the rhythm of technological advancement like a symphony. Each development is a note in a grander composition, contributing to a melody that resonates with progress and harmony. AI is the conductor of this orchestra, ensuring that every instrument—the Internet of things, big data, autonomous vehicles—plays in sync.

In literature, quotes often serve as windows into the soul of an idea. Alan Turing, the father of theoretical computer science and artificial intelligence, once posited, "Can machines think?" This question, simple in its wording, echoes through the corridors of time, challenging us to redefine the relationship between man and machine.

Show, don't tell. Imagine a child born into a world interwoven with AI, who never knows the drudgery of rote memorization or the frustration of unanswerable questions. For this child, AI is a friendly guide, a tireless tutor, always ready to explore the depths of human curiosity.

In this tapestry we weave, artificial intelligence is more than a mere thread; it is the loom shaping the fabric of our future. With AI as humanity's helping hand, we can craft a world limited only by the breadth of our imagination.

Imagine Virtual Reality as a Tool for Empathy

The quest for common ground has never been more urgent in a world brimming with diversity yet riddled with division. Daily headlines are saturated with stories of conflict born from a lack of understanding—a chasm between cultures, classes, and individuals. It's a reality that begs for a bridge, a conduit for empathy and connection.

Picture, if you will, a young woman named Sarah. She dons a headset, and suddenly, she's no longer in her cosy living room but walking the dusty streets of a war-torn city halfway across the globe. She can hear the distant sound of children's laughter, overshadowed by the ominous hum of drones overhead. This is the immersive power of virtual reality (VR), a technology that transports users into worlds beyond their own, fostering a profound sense of presence and empathy.

But what is this disconnect that we speak of, and why does it matter? At its core, the problem we're grappling with is a fundamental lack of empathy—the ability to understand and share the feelings of another. In a society where individualism often triumphs over community, it's easy to become ensconced in our bubbles, blind to the plights and joys of others. The consequences of such apathy are profound: societal polarization, discrimination, and a breeding ground for conflict.

What if we could step into the shoes of another, not metaphorically, but virtually? Enter VR, our proposed solution, a tool powerful enough to break down walls and build bridges of understanding. VR's immersive nature can simulate otherwise inaccessible experiences to most people, allowing them to experience life from a different perspective.

Implementing this technology as a tool for empathy involves a multi-step approach. First, we must create content that accurately and respectfully represents diverse perspectives. Next, we must ensure this technology is accessible to a broad audience, breaking the shackles of socioeconomic barriers. Educational programs, public installations, and partnerships with organizations are just a few avenues to bring VR into the mainstream consciousness.

Evidence of VR's ability to engender empathy is already coming to light. Studies have shown that after experiencing a VR simulation of colourblindness, individuals exhibit a greater understanding of the challenges faced by those with the condition. Similarly, VR experiences of homelessness have prompted users to take action, whether through donations or advocacy.

While VR stands out for its immersive qualities, it's not the only path to empathy. Traditional storytelling, social media campaigns, and community engagement programs also play pivotal roles. Yet, the unique power of VR lies in its ability to elicit visceral, emotional responses that can transform perceptions and behaviours.

Now, imagine the rhythmic beat of a heart pulsing with newfound understanding after a VR journey. Picture a world where the boundaries between 'your experience' and 'my experience' blur into 'our shared experience.' Such is the promise of VR as a tool for empathy.

Can we afford to ignore the potential of this technology? With every story shared, every life virtually lived, we weave a richer, more compassionate tapestry of human experience. VR is not just about escapism; it's about immersion into the realities of others and, in doing so, discovering the universal truths that bind us all.

A one-line paragraph for emphasis: In the landscape of human connection, VR is the lens that brings distant horizons into startling clarity.

Let's talk plainly: VR is not a silver bullet. It requires careful curation and ethical considerations to avoid voyeurism or oversimplification of complex issues. Yet, when wielded with care, VR can be a potent catalyst for empathy, a beacon guiding us toward a more understanding and unified society.

Consider the cadence of change, a dance between innovation and tradition. As VR takes its place in the choreography, we must embrace its rhythm, allowing it to enrich the previous movements.

To quote the famed virtual reality pioneer Jaron Lanier, "Virtual reality is the first medium that makes it possible for one person to walk a mile in another person's shoes." Indeed, VR has the power to break down barriers and open hearts, offering a glimpse into the lives of others with an immediacy that words alone cannot convey.

Show, don't tell. Imagine a world where conflicts are resolved not through force but through understanding, where policy is shaped by the lived experiences of people from all walks of life brought to life through VR. Imagine virtual reality as a window to new worlds and a mirror reflecting our shared humanity.

In this ongoing narrative, virtual reality emerges not merely as a technological marvel but as a vital instrument in the symphony of human empathy. With VR, we are no longer confined to the limits of our perspective; we are free to explore, understand, and imagine a world bound by empathy.

Imagine Robotics Elevating Quality of Life

In the ever-evolving tapestry of technological advancement, robotics emerges as a gleaming thread intertwined with the very fabric of human existence. Robots, once confined to the pages of science fiction, now stand shoulder to shoulder with us, poised to elevate our quality of life to unprecedented heights. But what does this integration truly entail, and how do the implications of robotics compare to the current human-led operations that shape our daily lives?

Picture a world where the sun never sets on productivity, where machines tirelessly tend to the tasks that once wearied human hands. In this realm, robotics is not merely a luxury but a cornerstone of societal function, addressing needs from the mundane to the critical with precision and unwavering endurance.

This book seeks to unravel the complex narrative woven by integrating robotics into our lives, dissecting the myriad ways these mechanical marvels parallel and diverge from human capabilities. By establishing a set of criteria encompassing efficiency, adaptability, and the emotional dimension of human-robot interaction, we delve into a balanced comparison that highlights both the harmonies and dissonances between man and machine.

The similarities that emerge are as fascinating as they are transformative. Robots, like humans, can be designed to learn, adapt, and execute tasks—yet they do so without succumbing to fatigue or the mercurial tides of emotion. In domains such as manufacturing, the parallels in task execution between robots and their human predecessors are striking, revealing a shared capacity for productivity that, in the case of robotics, is amplified by an unyielding consistency.

Yet, to view the landscape solely through the lens of similarity would be to ignore the rich contours that define the terrain. Robots differ from humans in their absence of innate empathy and nuanced judgment that comes from years of lived experience. A robot may excel in constructing a car or administering medication with impeccable accuracy, but can it comprehend the weight of responsibility or the joy of craftsmanship? This contrast is not merely academic; it shapes the very nature of how robots are integrated into workplaces, homes, and the broader society.

Visual aids are not merely supplementary but essential in crystallizing these comparisons for the reader. Graphs that contrast the error rates in tasks performed by humans and robots, or timelines showcasing the speed of robotic adoption across different industries, anchor the discourse in tangible reality.

The insights gleaned from this juxtaposition extend far beyond recognizing robots as efficient labourers. They provoke questions about the essence of human purpose and the allocation of value in a society where machines can outperform people in an expanding array of roles. What becomes of the human worker, the artisan, and the caregiver in this brave new world sculpted by silicon and steel?

How does this theoretical exploration align with the lived reality of contemporary society? Look around, and the signs of robotics' ascent are unmistakable. From automated checkouts in grocery stores to drones delivering medical supplies to remote communities, the real-world relevance of this discourse is undeniable. Each robotic intervention carries a ripple effect, altering job markets, reshaping industries, and redefining human interaction.

As we navigate through the intricate dance of progress, a question arises, almost unbidden: Are we prepared for the societal metamorphosis promised by the widespread adoption of robotics? It is a query that invites reflection, urging us to consider the practicalities of this technological evolution and its moral and ethical dimensions.

A one-sentence paragraph for emphasis: In the union of humans and robots, we find a mirror reflecting our highest aspirations and deepest anxieties.

The language of this exploration must be accessible, eschewing the esoteric in favour of a simplicity that invites understanding. It is a narrative punctuated by the rhythm of discovery, a cadence that echoes with the potential for both synergy and discord.

Perhaps it is through the words of Ada Lovelace, the prophetic mathematician who foresaw the computational revolution, that we find clarity: "The Analytical Engine has no pretensions to originate anything. It can do whatever we know how to order it to perform." Her vision encapsulates the heart of robotics—the tool that awaits our command, ready to elevate our quality of life, provided we wield it with wisdom and foresight.

Imagine a future where older people receive care from robots with a gentleness indistinguishable from human touch, where tedious labour is a relic of the past. Through the lens of robotics, we glimpse a world of boundless potential, a canvas awaiting the brushstrokes of human ingenuity.

This book is not merely an exposition of what is but an invitation to dream of what could be. In the nuanced interplay between humans and robots, we encounter a symphony of progress, each note resonating with the promise of an elevated quality of life. Imagine the crescendo of a society where robotics and humanity harmonize in a masterpiece of collective well-being.

Imagine Global Connectivity Bridging Minds

In the intricate web of our interconnected world, the tendrils of global connectivity have woven a tapestry of shared understanding that transcends borders and oceans. It is a realm where ideas flow as seamlessly as rivers, nurturing the landscapes of our collective consciousness. This story is not just of transformation; it's a chronicle of the unity that global connectivity has fostered among diverse minds across the planet.

In the early days, communication was bound by the constraints of physical proximity. Messages were carried by foot, horseback, or sailing vessel, taking weeks or months to reach their destination. The inception of global connectivity can be traced back to the advent of the telegraph in the 19th century, a revolution that compressed time and space, making instant communication a startling new reality.

The milestones that punctuate the history of global connectivity are both numerous and momentous. From laying the first transatlantic telegraph cable in 1858 to the birth of the internet in the late 20th century, each leap forward brought humanity closer together. The creation of the World Wide Web in 1989 was a watershed moment, forever altering how knowledge was shared and absorbed.

Visual aids, such as timelines illustrating the exponential growth of internet users or infographics displaying the surge of data exchanged daily, crystallize this evolution's magnitude. These tools are not mere embellishments but are vital to understanding the rapid pace at which our world has become interlinked.

Cultural and regional variations in the adoption and impact of global connectivity are as rich as they are instructive. In some parts of the world, the internet has empowered grassroots movements and democratized information; in others, it has become a tool for surveillance and control. The narrative of connectivity is not one-size-fits-all; it is a patchwork of stories, each coloured by the hues of local norms and values.

Turning our gaze to modern interpretations and adaptations, we witness an era where social media platforms have become the new town squares, and digital nomadism is no longer a fringe lifestyle but a mainstream choice. The proliferation of smartphones has put the power of the internet in the palms of our hands, making global connectivity a constant companion.

Yet, this story is not without its challenges and controversies. The digital divide remains a stark reality, with billions still disconnected from the online world. Issues like data privacy, cyberbullying, and the spread of misinformation have surfaced as turning points, demanding our attention and action. These are not mere footnotes in the history of global connectivity; they are critical junctures that shape its trajectory.

Do you ever pause to consider how this vast interconnected network affects your life, thoughts, and relationships? Have you ever stopped asking yourself what it truly means to be a global citizen in a world where distance has lost meaning?

In a single, resonant sentence, let it be said: Connectivity is the modern canvas on which our collective destiny is painted—a continuously evolving picture with each of us holding a brush.

Our language must be clear, for the story of global connectivity is not reserved for the technocrats but belongs to us all. It dances with a rhythm felt in every corner of the globe, a cadence that speaks of unity amidst diversity.

In the words of cultural anthropologist Margaret Mead, "Never doubt that a small group of thoughtful, committed citizens can change the world; indeed, it's the only thing that ever has." Global connectivity has amplified this sentiment, proving that shared ideas can spark movements that reshape our societies.

Imagine a future where every individual has the means to contribute to the global dialogue, where the exchange of cultural insights leads to a more prosperous, more empathetic world community. As the lines between local and international blur, we find ourselves at the cusp of a new chapter in human history, where the barriers that once divided us give way to bridges of understanding.

This narrative is not a mere recounting of technological milestones; it is an invitation to envision and shape a future where global connectivity is the cornerstone of a world built on the pillars of knowledge, empathy, and inclusivity. Each note resonates with the potential for a more enlightened and united human experience in the harmonious symphony of interconnected minds. Imagine the symphony of a world where every mind is connected, every voice heard, and every heart understood.

Imagine Medicine Tailored to Every Individual

Imagine a world where an arsenal of genetic data accompanies the white coats and stethoscopes of today's doctors, each patient's unique blueprint guiding the hands that heal. The convergence of biology, technology, and data science has birthed an era of medicine so precise and personalized that it may seem like science fiction. Yet, this is the dawn of a new paradigm in healthcare, where treatments and preventions are tailored to the individual's genetic makeup, lifestyle, and even their environment.

At the heart of this revolution lies a simple yet profound claim: that every person is unique, and so should their medical care. This assertion is not without merit, for the evidence mounts with each passing day. We've witnessed the success of targeted cancer therapies, where drugs are designed to attack specific mutations found in a patient's tumour. This form of treatment, known as precision oncology, has transformed the prognosis for many, turning what was once a death sentence into a manageable condition.

Delve more profoundly, and you'll find a treasure trove of data supporting this personalized approach. Clinical trials have shown that patients with certain genetic markers respond better to specific medications, leading to fewer adverse reactions and more effective treatment outcomes. Advances in genomic sequencing make it possible to decode an individual's DNA at a fraction of the cost and time it once took, paving the way for bespoke medical care.

But let us not don a rose-coloured lens without acknowledging the shadows it casts. Sceptics rightfully point out that personalized medicine is not without its challenges. The ethical dilemmas of genetic privacy, the potential for discrimination by insurers or employers, and the staggering costs associated with these advanced treatments—are but a few of the counterpoints raised in opposition. There's also the concern that, despite our advances, we may only be scratching the surface of understanding the complex interplay between genetics, environment, and disease.

In response, proponents of personalized medicine argue that the benefits far outweigh the risks. They clarify that with robust legal frameworks, the issues of privacy and discrimination can be mitigated. Moreover, as technology advances and becomes more widespread, costs will likely decrease, as in other technology areas. The hope is that, in time, personalized medicine will not only be more effective but also more accessible.

Additional evidence points to the growing field of pharmacogenomics, where genetic information guides the selection of drugs to maximize efficacy and minimize harm. This is not the medicine of tomorrow, but today, with certain hospitals and clinics already integrating genetic testing into their standard of care for specific conditions.

As we conclude, let us reinforce the assertion that personalized medicine stands on solid ground with its promise of treatments tailored to the individual. The future it heralds is one of hope—a future where the battle against illness is as singular as the DNA that defines us.

Imagine the day you walk into a clinic, and the treatment you receive is designed exclusively for you. It's a future where the phrase "Take two of these and call me in the morning" is replaced by "This has been made just for you." This is not a distant dream but a tangible reality unfolding before our eyes.

In the eloquent words of a pioneer in the field, "Personalized medicine is the art of the possible. It's not about playing God, but about using the tools He has given us to heal as He would—individually, compassionately, effectively."

Picture, then, a world where each patient's story is not just heard but is also central to their care—a world where medicine is as individual as a fingerprint. This is the world of personalized medicine, and it's within our grasp. Imagine, imagine, the symphony of healing that could unfold when every treatment is a note tailored to the patient's biological melody.

The Wealth of Well-being

Imagine Work-Life Balance Achieved Globally

In the dim glow of dawn, a father laces up his sneakers for an early morning jog, the first of many choices reflecting a global shift. It's a world where the once elusive equilibrium between the grindstone and the hearth is no longer a mere fantasy. This is a new reality—a work-life balance achieved globally, a tapestry woven from the threads of countless individuals' lives, intertwining personal happiness and professional fulfilment.

Beneath the veneer of this idyllic scene, a significant issue once festered, threatening to undermine the social fabric of societies worldwide. The modern workforce, shackled to their desks and digital devices, had been plagued by the relentless demand for productivity at the expense of well-being. The 24/7 work culture, glorified for generations, came at a steep cost—burnout, strained relationships, and many health issues.

If left unchecked, this imbalance promised a bleak future. We stood on the precipice of a world where children would grow up recognizing their parents by their furrowed brows, illuminated by the cold glow of a laptop rather than the warmth of shared experiences. The consequences of inaction painted a dire picture: a decrease in life expectancy, a rise in mental health crises, and the erosion of the very societal cornerstones—family, community, and leisure—that make life worth living.

The solution was multifaceted, emerging like a phoenix from the ashes of countless burnt-out careers. It required a bold reimagining of work culture, spearheaded by a movement that valued employees as people, not just cogs in a corporate machine. Flexible hours, telecommuting, and a redefined measure of success that included mental health and happiness became the new norm.

Implementing these changes was no small feat. It began with a cultural revolution where CEOs and policymakers championed the cause, implementing laws and policies protecting work-life balance. Corporations introduced mandatory time-off policies and limited overtime, while technology was harnessed to automate menial tasks, freeing up time for creative and strategic thinking.

Evidence of this transformation's efficacy was not long in revealing itself. Studies showcased a surge in productivity, reduced healthcare costs due to stress-related illnesses, and a revitalization of community engagement as people rediscovered the time to invest in their localities and hobbies.

Yet, one solution does not fit all. Alternative approaches were considered, such as introducing a four-day workweek, sabbaticals for long-term employees, and the concept of 'job-sharing' for roles that permitted it. Each option held merit and underscored the necessity for tailored solutions catering to diverse industries and individual needs.

As you ponder this new world, consider the jogger once more. His footsteps are light, his breath steady. He runs not to escape the day ahead but to savour a moment of solitude before embracing the promise of a balanced life. The streets are quiet, but they thrum with the potential of a day where work serves life, not vice versa.

Can you envision a day when the 9-to-5 shackles are a relic of the past? When your work is a single brushstroke on the canvas of your life, not the entire masterpiece?

The journey to this utopia was not without its sceptics. Detractors claimed it was a fanciful dream, incompatible with economic growth and global competitiveness. But the proof lay in the thriving communities, the laughter of children playing with parents unburdened by the weight of work after hours, and the innovation sparked by well-rested minds.

In conclusion, the global achievement of work-life balance is not a mere flight of fancy. It results from deliberate actions, a collective will to prioritize humanity over blind production. It is a testament to what can be accomplished when the world dares to imagine—and then dares to act.

The father returns from his run, his children greeting him with sleepy smiles, the day ahead full of possibility. This is the world we've created. This is the world we live in. This is the world we imagined.

Imagine Mental Health No Longer Taboo

Imagine a society where the murmur of conversation about mental health flows as freely as discussions about the latest sports scores or the weather. Visualize a time and place where the mind is treated with the same reverence and concern as the body, where a trip to a therapist is as routine as a visit to a dentist, and where emotional well-being is woven into the fabric of daily life.

In the pages that follow, we will embark on an exploration of this very idea, dissecting concepts that are integral to a deeper comprehension of mental health. We will delve into the meanings of words like stigma, therapy, and resilience, unravelling their significance to fully grasp the tapestry of a world-embracing mental well-being without hesitation.

Let us commence with a curated compendium of terms that will serve as the bedrock for our journey. Included in this list are stigma, therapy, resilience, mindfulness, depression, anxiety, bipolar disorder, schizophrenia, and self-care. Each of these terms, though perhaps familiar, carries a weight of importance that is often overlooked or misunderstood.

Stigma, a mark of disgrace associated with a particular circumstance, quality, or person, often shadows mental health. Yet, imagine a world where this stigma dissolves, where compassion replaces judgment and understanding supplants fear. Here, the term is stripped of its power to isolate and instead becomes a catalyst for conversation and change.

Therapy, intended to relieve or heal a disorder, frequently conjures images of couches and notepads. However, its essence lies in the therapeutic relationship—a bond of trust and understanding that serves as a beacon of hope for those navigating the tumultuous seas of mental distress.

Resilience, the capacity to recover quickly from difficulties, is a testament to the human spirit's indefatigable nature. Envision a society that cultivates resilience, empowering individuals to rise from adversity with renewed strength and wisdom.

Mindfulness, a mental state achieved by focusing one's awareness on the present moment, offers a sanctuary from the relentless pace of modern life. It beckons us to pause, breathe, and engage with our surroundings with intention and grace.

Depression, a common but serious mood disorder, casts a long shadow over the lives of many. In our reimagined world, depression is not a whispered secret but a challenge met with support and a wealth of resources to guide those affected toward the light of recovery.

Anxiety, a feeling of worry or unease, often goes unacknowledged, mistaken for mere stress. Yet, peeling back the layers, we find a complex condition deserving attention and care.

Bipolar disorder and schizophrenia, both misunderstood and stigmatized, represent the spectrum of mental health conditions that are often relegated to the shadows. By bringing these into the light, we acknowledge the diverse experiences of mental health and the varied paths to wellness.

Self-care, the practice of taking action to preserve or improve one's health, is the cornerstone of a society that values mental health. It is the recognition that maintaining our well-being is not an act of indulgence but a vital component of a fulfilling life.

What if these terms were not merely words but bridges to understanding, fostering empathy instead of alienation? Can you envisage a world where children are taught the language of emotions as fluently as their ABCs, where the workplace champions mental health days, and community centres offer workshops on coping skills?

As you absorb these definitions, picture the faces of those around you. Each carries an invisible narrative rich with struggles, triumphs, fears, and dreams. We humanize the concepts by connecting these definitions to the faces of our friends, family, and even strangers. We remind ourselves that behind every term is a person, a life touched by the ebbs and flows of mental health.

Such a world is within reach. It is a place where the chains of stigma fall away, where the light of knowledge and acceptance dispels the shadows of ignorance. In this world, the language of mental health is spoken with the same ease and normality as any other topic of human health and well-being.

Envision that you are not alone in your contemplation of this new reality. Imagine that millions are joining you in this reflection across the globe, each a ripple in the vast ocean of change. Together, these ripples merge to form waves of transformation, reshaping the landscape of mental health and erasing the taboo that has long silenced our collective voice.

Let this be the world we strive for, the world we create, the world we imagine.

Imagine Communities Built on Mutual Support

Amid the hum of a vibrant marketplace, where the scent of spices intertwines with the laughter of children, lies the heart of a remarkable community—a place where mutual support is not just an ideal but the very foundation of existence. This is the setting of our story, a canvas painted with the delicate brushstrokes of human connection and interdependence.

In this enclave, we meet the main players: Aisha, a wise elder with a gentle smile that belies her steely resolve; Carlos, a young teacher whose innovative ideas ripple through the community; and Maya, an entrepreneur whose business serves not only as a source of income but also as a hub of collaboration and growth. Each character embodies the spirit of the community, with their stories intricately woven into the rich tapestry of this social experiment.

The challenge they face is not unique—a need for sustainable living in a world where resources are often scarce, and the well-being of individuals can be overlooked. Yet, here in this community, the issue takes on a different hue, coloured by the shared belief in the strength of unity and mutual aid.

The approach to overcoming this challenge is both innovative and steeped in tradition. The community members pool their skills and resources in a system of exchange and support that transcends mere transactional relationships. Aisha's knowledge of traditional medicine, Carlos's gift for education, and Maya's entrepreneurial acumen become communal assets rather than individual possessions.

The results of this symbiotic strategy are remarkable. Where once there were needs unmet and potential untapped, now there is a flourishing of opportunity and a sense of collective accomplishment. Data, though difficult to quantify in the currency of the heart, shows a marked increase in the community's overall health, educational attainment, and economic stability.

Yet, the journey is not without its critics—voices from outside and within that question the scalability or the sustainability of such a model. Reflecting on these concerns, the community recognizes that the beauty of their system lies not in its perfection but in its adaptability and resilience.

Visual aids, like the communal garden that serves as both a source of nourishment and a classroom, make the concept tangible. The intertwining vines of tomatoes and beans become a metaphor for the interwoven lives of the community members.

Drawing back to the larger narrative, this case study is more than an isolated instance of success; it is a microcosm of what could be a beacon for a world yearning for connection and mutual respect.

As the sun dips below the horizon and the marketplace slowly empties, a thought lingers in the air—a question that beckons each of us to consider our role in the greater whole: What if the world embraced the principles of mutual support as readily as this community? What transformations could we witness in societies torn by division and strife?

In a world often dominated by competition and self-interest, the very notion of mutual support as a guiding principle can seem like a distant dream. Yet, as I reflect on my journey—from the bustling streets of Tehran to the orderly calm of Copenhagen, and finally, to the pulsing heart of London—I am reminded that the seeds of community and mutual support are universal. They are sown in the fertile ground of our shared humanity, watered by the simple yet profound acts of kindness that transcend cultural and geographic boundaries.

As we close the pages of this chapter, let us carry with us the spirit of Aisha, Carlos, and Maya. Let their stories inspire us to forge bonds of support with those around us, to build communities not of isolation but of inclusion. In this world, every individual feels valued, empowered, and part of something greater than themselves.

Imagine Education That Nurtures Individuality

In the annals of history, there was a time when education was not a system but an organic process. Imagine stepping into the groves of ancient Greece, where philosophers like Plato and Aristotle engaged with their students under the dappled sunlight, fostering dialogue and debate. It was a place and time where learning was synonymous with personal growth and self-discovery.

As centuries advanced, so too did our approach to education. The Industrial Revolution, a turning point in human history, brought a paradigm shift. Schools mirrored the factories, focusing on uniformity and efficiency. Students became products on a conveyor belt, each subjected to the same process, hoping to achieve a standard result. This model, once revolutionary in its capacity to educate the masses, now stands as a relic of an age where conformity was the currency of survival.

Fast forward to the present, where the echoes of those factory whistles still linger in the hallways of our schools. The world has transformed into a kaleidoscope of technology and innovation. Yet, many classrooms remain moored to the past, adhering to a one-size-fits-all mentality that fails to recognize the brilliant spectrum of human capability.

Why, one might ask, does history matter now? Because the world we navigate today is the result of our educational roots. To change course, we must understand the journey that brought us here. In a society increasingly defined by rapid and complex challenges, can we afford to overlook the unique talents and interests that each learner brings to the table?

Imagine a canvas as yet unpainted, awaiting the first stroke of a visionary brush. Here, in the fertile ground between past and present, our story unfolds—a narrative of transformation and hope.

Within these pages, we do not merely recount tales of what is, but rather, we dare to envision what could be. What if classrooms were ecosystems, vibrant with diversity, where each student's individuality was not just acknowledged but celebrated? Picture a place where education is not about memorizing facts but about igniting passions, where the metric of success is not a test score but the joy of learning.

Do you remember when curiosity propelled you forward when learning was not a chore but an adventure? This is the very essence we seek to recapture. It is a call to foster an education that adapts to the learner rather than forcing the learner to adjust.

Imagine a young girl, her eyes alight with wonder as she dismantles a clock, her hands deftly exploring the cogs and springs that dictate its rhythm. Or a boy, lost in the lines of a poem, finding solace and understanding in the cadence of the words. These are not mere daydreams but the beginnings of a movement, a shift from the industrial model to a renaissance of individualized learning.

And what of the teachers? They are the gardeners in this metaphorical landscape, cultivating potential, nurturing growth, and taking pride not in the uniformity of their crops but in the rich variety that blooms. Their role is pivotal, for they are not just transmitters of knowledge but guides in a journey of discovery.

Each chapter that follows is a testament to this vision. We will explore the stories of educators who have dared to challenge the status quo, students who have found their voice in the chorus of education, and communities that have been strengthened by recognising individual gifts.

In a world that often feels fragmented, education has the power to be a unifying force. By embracing the unique talents of each learner, we can create a tapestry of capabilities that is far greater than the sum of its parts.

Imagine a future where education is not a barrier but a bridge, not a trial but a triumph. This is the journey we embark upon—a quest to reshape learning, to honour the individual, and to craft a legacy that will endure for generations to come.

Then, with open minds and hopeful hearts, let us enter this new chapter. For it is in our power to sculpt an education that breathes life into every child's imagination, cherishes each learner's distinct song, and prepares a symphony of minds to dance to the complex rhythms of our world. Let us imagine together.

Imagine Ageing With Grace and Dignity

Imagine, if you will, a world where each wrinkle tells a story of laughter, every silver hair a testament to the wisdom gathered, and every step taken a dance of life's rich tapestry. As we embark on this journey through the pages of "Imagine Ageing with Grace and Dignity," we delve into the heart of what it means to grow older with respect, to cherish the process, and to view the autumn of life as a season filled with its unique beauty.

Our society often paints ageing in a light that dims the vibrancy of those experiencing it. But within this narrative, we aim to shift the perspective, cast a glow on the golden years, and present a list of core values that honour older people as they continue to bloom with grace and dignity.

:

In the following pages, we assemble a collection of foundational elements that underscore the importance of embracing ageing as a natural and enriching stage of life. This enumeration is not merely a set of abstract concepts; it is the scaffolding upon which we can build a more compassionate and respectful culture for our seniors.

:

The list includes the following pivotal points: Celebrating Wisdom, Fostering Independence, Encouraging Connectivity, Cultivating Contentment, and Embracing Legacy.

:

Wisdom is the crown jewel of ageing, an amalgamation of experience, knowledge, and insight.

:

As we explore the concept of wisdom, we uncover the layers of life lessons accrued over decades. These are the pearls of practical advice, the strategies for emotional resilience, and the quiet understanding of life's complexities that only time can teach.

:

Through interviews with octogenarians and nonagenarians, we unearth stories of decisions made with foresight and the guidance offered to younger generations. Scholars and historians also remind us that elders are revered as living libraries in many cultures, their advice sought in matters ranging from family to governance.

:

In practical terms, celebrating wisdom means creating platforms for intergenerational dialogue, integrating the insights of older people in community planning, and valuing their perspectives in family decisions.

:

Maintaining autonomy is crucial to ageing with dignity.

:

Independence in older age encompasses the ability to make choices about one's daily life, from the mundane to the monumental. It involves access to resources that support self-sufficiency and the agency to live according to one's values and desires.

:

Studies in gerontology consistently show that seniors who feel in control of their lives report higher levels of satisfaction and better health outcomes. Personal narratives from individuals who have successfully navigated the balance between independence and support provide a blueprint for others.

:

Practical support for independence might include adaptive technologies for the home, community-based assistance programs, and healthcare that prioritizes patient choice.

:

Social connections are the threads that bind the fabric of our lives and are crucial in our later years.

:

Connectivity for the elderly is more than preventing loneliness; it's about maintaining a sense of belonging, contribution, and joy. It's about preserving the ties to family, friends, and community that imbue life with meaning.

:

Research demonstrates that a robust social network can reduce the risks of cognitive decline and depression in the elderly. Heartwarming accounts of seniors who remain active in social groups, volunteer work, or even online communities illustrate the vibrancy that connectivity can bring.

:

To encourage connectivity, we can develop community programs that are inclusive of all ages, promote senior-friendly technology, and support transportation options that keep the elderly engaged with their surroundings.

:

Contentment in ageing is the art of finding satisfaction in the present moment, of appreciating the journey thus far and the simple pleasures that each day can bring.

:

Contentment is not about complacency but a deep-seated sense of peace from within. It's about accepting life's ebbs and flows and savouring the sweetness amid the bitters.

:

Psychological research points to gratitude and mindfulness practices as keys to contentment at any age. Tales from those who have mastered the art of contentment in their later years often feature a gratitude practice or a mindful approach to daily life.

:

To cultivate contentment, we can encourage practices such as gratitude journals, meditation, and community activities that focus on the present experience rather than past achievements or future worries.

:

Legacy is the unique imprint we leave on the world, and embracing it is about recognizing and celebrating the impact of one's life.

:

Embracing legacy involves both looking back with pride at one's contributions and looking forward to the influence that continues through stories, traditions, and values passed on. It's about acknowledging that every life is a story worth sharing.

:

Biographies and family histories offer powerful examples of legacies treasured and preserved. Projecting these stories into the future, we see how one person's lived experience can impact subsequent generations.

:

Embracing legacy can take the form of recording oral histories, creating legacy projects with grandchildren, or simply sharing life lessons with others.

In conclusion, it is not just an invitation to rethink our approach to ageing; it is a call to action. It urges us to weave these principles into the fabric of our daily lives, ensuring that as we or our loved ones journey through the later years, it is done with the respect and celebration that every person deserves. As we turn each page, let us remember that the beauty of life does not diminish with age; it simply evolves into a new phase of wonder and richness.

Compassionate Governance

Imagine Leaders Who Truly Serve the People

In the heart of a bustling city, where the clamour of daily life crescendos like the fervent symphony of an orchestra, there stood a man apart. This man—let's call him Kian— gazed upon the parliament buildings with eyes that held the weight of hope, eyes that had seen the people's struggles and yearned for a new dawn. His hands, calloused from years of labour, were now tools of change, grasping the fabric of society's needs with a gentle yet firm touch.

Kian's story was not written in the annals of history books nor celebrated with fanfare and adulation. His was a quiet revolution that began in the forgotten alleyways where the destitute whispered their dreams to the uncaring night. Here, among the discarded aspirations of a generation, Kian found his calling—not in the halls of power but in the heart of service.

As the sun descended, casting a golden hue over the city, Kian walked among the people he had come to serve. Each step was a commitment, each gesture a promise unspoken.

His was not the charismatic flamboyance of a seasoned politician; rather, he embodied the unassuming grace of a true servant leader.

Why, one might ask, would a man of such potential choose the path less trodden, the road paved with sacrifice and silent victories? The answer lay in the stories etched upon the faces of those he met. A single mother, toiling away to feed her children in the absence of a state that had promised much but delivered little. An elderly man whose wrinkled hands held the broken dreams of his youth, now seeking only the comfort of a community that had long since fractured.

"Do you see them?" Kian would often murmur to no one in particular, his voice barely rising above the din of the city. "These are the souls we are meant to serve, the lives we are entrusted to better."

And so, Kian embarked on an unexpected journey, one that challenged the very fabric of political ambition. He listened more than he spoke, learned more than he taught, and, in doing so, he began to weave a new narrative—one that echoed with the voices of the unheard.

Could a leader truly set aside ego and ambition for the greater good? Could empathy and integrity be more than just words inscribed on the dusty shelves of idealism? Kian believed so, and with each passing day, his belief took root in the hearts of those around him.

A hush fell over the city as the moon appeared in the night sky. In that moment of tranquillity, Kian's vision seemed to permeate the air the city's denizens breathed. It was a vision of a world where leaders were guardians of the public's trust, stewards of a collective future.

"Imagine," he whispered into the night, "a place where those elected to lead with a servant's heart, where power is not hoarded but shared, where every decision is drenched in the deep well of compassion."

It was a simple yet profound revelation. And within this revelation lay the wisdom that the readers of this book would uncover, page by page, chapter by chapter. An understanding of a new paradigm, where leadership was not a ladder to personal glory but a pathway to communal prosperity.

In the quietude of that night, as Kian contemplated the journey ahead, one question lingered in the air, unspoken yet palpable: How might our world transform if such leaders were not figments of our imagination but the architects of our reality?

This was the promise of Kian's story—a beacon of what could be, an invitation to explore the boundless potential of the human spirit when guided by selflessness and devotion to the common good. The challenge was set, the gauntlet thrown down to everyone who dared to dream of a better tomorrow.

And so, dear reader, consider this as you turn each page: What might you do to contribute to this vision? How can you, in your own way, become a leader who truly serves? Let us embark on this journey with open hearts and minds, ready to be inspired, learn, and ultimately act.

Imagine a Global Consensus on Climate Action

The seeds of change, often sown in the unlikeliest places, can blossom into a forest of renewal and hope. This is the story of how disparate nations, historically divided by invisible lines on maps and the tangible schisms of ideology, came together to form a global consensus on climate action—a tale as intricate and evolving as the roots of an ancient tree.

Once, the subject of climate change was a mere whisper in the annals of scientific circles, a spectre on the horizon that few chose to acknowledge. It began as a theory postulated by scholars and researchers who peered into the murky depths of climate patterns and fossil records.

The earliest origins of climate action can be traced back to the late 19th century when scientists first proposed that human activities could influence climate and weather patterns. However, it wasn't until the latter half of the 20th century that the clarion call of climate change began to echo with more urgency through the halls of power and public consciousness.

123

Key milestones are followed chronologically, like stepping stones across an ever-widening river. The formation of the Intergovernmental Panel on Climate Change (IPCC) in 1988 marked a pivotal moment, as did the Earth Summit in Rio de Janeiro in 1992, which led to the adoption of the United Nations Framework Convention on Climate Change (UNFCCC).

As we leaf through the pages of history, visual aids in the form of graphs show the steady rise in global temperatures, the melting of ice caps, and the increasing levels of greenhouse gas emissions. These images, stark and unforgiving, have enhanced our understanding and underscored the urgency of the matter at hand.

Cultural and regional variations in the evolution of climate action are evident. Some nations, blessed with abundant resources, took early strides toward renewable energy and sustainable practices. Others, constrained by economic hardship or political strife, lagged behind, their contributions to global emissions dwarfed by their struggle for survival.

Recent developments have seen a surge in modern interpretations and adaptations of climate action. Innovative technologies for carbon capture, advancements in renewable energy, and a burgeoning consciousness in consumer behaviour have been the harbingers of hope in a world teetering on the brink of ecological collapse.

Yet, the path has been strewn with challenges, controversies, and turning points. The withdrawal of certain nations from international agreements, debates over the economic implications of climate policies, and the rise of climate denialism have all served as stark reminders that the road to consensus is fraught with obstacles.

Do we possess the collective will to overcome these hurdles? The answer lies not in the rhetoric of the past but in the actions we choose to take today.

In the current climate, nations have begun to recognize the undeniable truth—that none can stand alone in the face of this global threat. The conversation is changing in boardrooms and parliaments, streets, and schools. Climate action is no longer deemed a hindrance to progress; rather, it is the engine driving us toward a more sustainable future.

The turning point came, not with a bang, but with a realization that whispered through the corridors of power and echoed in the chambers of the United Nations. It was a moment of clarity, born from the ashes of wildfires and the ravages of hurricanes. It was the moment the world declared, in one voice, "Enough."

Imagine, then, a world where this global consensus is not a fleeting dream but a living, breathing reality. The leaders of nations convene, not to argue over the pieces of a shrinking pie but to share in creating a banquet that all can enjoy—a sustainable feast for generations to come.

Can you see it? A future where the air is clean, the oceans are vibrant with life, and the forests stand tall and proud. It is a vision that requires the minds of our greatest thinkers and the hearts of every individual.

As we stand at the crossroads of history, one question remains, echoing through the annals of time: Will we rise to meet the challenge of our age and forge a legacy of unity and action?

This is the essence of our story, a narrative woven from the threads of countless efforts and unyielding determination—a tapestry of human ingenuity and collective will. It is the story of 'Imagine a Global Consensus on Climate Action,' a chronicle of the world as it could be if only we dare to make it so.

And so, dear reader, consider your role in this grand design as you ponder the pages before you. How will you contribute to the fabric of this global consensus? Let us walk together, hand in hand, into a future where our actions today become the heritage of tomorrow. Let us imagine, and then let us act.

Imagine Education as a Universal Right

In a world where knowledge is the key to unlocking a future of possibilities, imagine a landscape where education is not a privilege but a fundamental right for every child, every adult, and every person—irrespective of their birthplace, economic status, or social standing. Imagine a horizon where the luminous glow of enlightenment eradicates the shadows of ignorance and inequality.

As we delve into the annals of history, it becomes apparent that education, or the lack thereof, has been the cornerstone upon which societies have either flourished or floundered. The disparity in educational access has carved deep trenches in the fabric of civilization, with the privileged few basking in the light of knowledge and the less fortunate languishing in the darkness of illiteracy and missed opportunity.

Now, let us confront the issue at its core: education, a basic human right as declared by the United Nations, is still not within the grasp of millions. Many children, by sheer accident of geography or circumstance, are denied the ladder to climb out of poverty, challenge their intellect, and dream of a better life.

What will become of a world that turns its back on this stark reality? If left unaddressed, the consequences are dire: an unskilled workforce, increased vulnerability to socio-economic shocks, a widening gender gap, and the most egregious of all—the untapped potential of countless human minds.

But within this bleak panorama lies the seed of transformation. The solution is as straightforward as it is ambitious: make education universally accessible, free at the point of delivery, an unassailable right for all. This is not mere idealism but a tangible goal, one that requires a global commitment to funding, infrastructure, and policy reform.

Implementing such a solution is a mosaic of complex but achievable steps. It begins with investment, not as charity but as the most prudent of expenditures. It continues with the construction of schools, the training of teachers, the development of inclusive curricula, and the integration of technology to bridge the distances that keep knowledge at bay.

Evidence of success glimmers on the horizon—countries that have embraced education for all have seen dramatic increases in literacy rates, economic growth, and societal health. Imagine a young girl in a remote village attending school for the first time, her potential no longer shackled by circumstance. This is the outcome we strive for, the victory we can claim.

Of course, alternative solutions exist: scholarship programs, non-governmental education initiatives, and community-led efforts. Each of these plays a vital role, and yet, without the unequivocal backing of universal education as a right, they are but stopgaps in a system in need of overhaul.

Imagine, then, a world where every child can sit in a classroom, where knowledge is a gift given freely, and where the chains of ignorance are broken by the power of education. Imagine a society unfettered by the constraints of illiteracy, where every person has the opportunity to contribute to the greater good.

This is not a fantasy but a future within our reach—a future where the collective will of humanity rises to affirm that education is not just a pathway but a right. It is a vision that demands our attention, dedication, and unyielding effort.

So let us ask ourselves: What world do we want to create? Will we accept the status quo, or will we dare to imagine—

and realize—a world where education opens every door, for everyone, everywhere?

The narrative of education as a universal right is not yet complete, but with each step we take toward this ideal, we write a new chapter in the annals of human progress. Let us be the generation that turns the dream of universal education into a resounding reality. In the imagining, we sow the seeds for a future that can—and must—come to pass.

Imagine Justice Systems Rooted in Rehabilitation

Emerging from the realms of education, one cannot help but ponder the interconnectedness of our society's institutions. The justice system, a mosaic of laws, penalties, and rehabilitation programs, is a pillar of societal order. Yet, within its walls lies a stark divergence of philosophies: one rooted in retribution, the other in rehabilitation. Let us embark on a journey through these contrasting ideologies, exploring their textures and seeking insights into how they shape our world.

In this narrative, we draw the lens closer to the justice systems that envelop our society, like the ivy on an ancient edifice. The purpose is clear: to dissect the intricate weave of punishment and rehabilitation, understanding how each influences the individual and the community.

To establish a fair comparison, we must first lay down the criteria—recidivism rates, societal impact, cost-effectiveness, and the moral implications of each approach. As our gaze shifts between these benchmarks, a tapestry of similarities and distinctions emerges, each thread revealing more about the ideals we uphold.

The similarities between punitive and rehabilitative approaches are sometimes more than mere coincidence; both, at their core, seek to deter crime and ensure public safety. Yet, how they achieve these ends diverges like rivers from a single source. Where punitive measures lean heavily on the scales of justice, tipping towards the weight of penalties, rehabilitation seeks to restore to rebuild the individual beyond their transgression.

The contrasts, however, are stark and telling. Punitive systems often rely on incarceration—a blunt tool that removes the offender from society but does little to address the underlying causes of their behaviour. Rehabilitation, on the other hand, embraces the notion of transformation. It is the gentle hand that guides rather than the iron fist that punishes.

Visual aids, though not present in this text, could clarify this dichotomy. Graphs showing recidivism rates plummeting in rehabilitative programs or charts delineating the cost savings when reformative practices are employed would offer concrete evidence of the benefits of such an approach.

Delving deeper into this analysis, we uncover profound insights. Rehabilitation serves the individual and weaves a more robust social fabric. It fosters empathy, encourages community involvement, and promotes a more humane society. The broader implications cannot be overstated: a rehabilitative justice system can potentially transform lives and entire communities.

Contemporary relevance is found in countries that have already made strides towards prioritizing rehabilitation. In these places, former offenders find new paths as productive members of society, the cycle of crime is interrupted, and the narrative of justice is rewritten.

But where does this leave us, the observers, the thinkers, the dreamers of better worlds? Can we fathom a justice system that holds at its heart the promise of redemption and the potential for second chances? Do we dare to imagine?

Imagine a young man, once on the wrong side of the law, now a beacon of change in his community. His journey through a rehabilitative program is one of struggle and triumph—a testament to the power of transformation. This is not merely an anecdote; it is a possibility made real by the embrace of a justice system that heals rather than harms.

And yet, our prose must not descend into the abyss of naivety. We must recognize the complexity of crime and the necessity of consequences. But even within this recognition, we find space for questions, for contemplation. What if, instead of asking, 'How should they pay?', we ponder, 'How can they change?'

A one-line paragraph for emphasis: Imagine justice as a pathway to redemption.

In our quest for simplicity, let us not conflate it with simplification. The issues at hand are nuanced and multifaceted, demanding thoughtful consideration and deliberate action. But the essence remains clear: rehabilitation offers a future that punitive measures cannot—a future where the potential is not squandered behind bars but nurtured in the light of opportunity.

The rhythm of our society and the cadence of our collective action must resonate with the values we cherish. Through a blend of reflective contemplation and decisive action, we can craft a justice system that mirrors our highest ideals.

Quotes from reformers and dialogues from those who have walked the path of rehabilitation add richness and authenticity to our narrative, painting a picture of the transformative power of second chances.

We must show, not just tell, the benefits of a justice system rooted in rehabilitation. Through examples, anecdotes, and descriptive language, we can illuminate the path toward a more restorative approach to justice—one that values human dignity and fosters societal harmony.

As we close this chapter, let us hold fast to the vision of a justice system where rehabilitation stands as the cornerstone. For in the imagining of such a world, we lay the groundwork for a future where justice and compassion walk hand in hand. Imagine, then, a society where every fall is met with a helping hand, where every transgression is an opportunity for growth, where justice serves not as the end of a journey but as the beginning of a new chapter in the story of a life reclaimed.

Imagine Political Decisions Driven by Future Generations

Imagine a society that shapes the very fabric of its legacy, a world where political choices are etched with the foresight of centuries to come. As you delve into the pages of this book, you are not merely embarking on a journey through ideas and propositions; you are stepping into a realm where the future breathes life into every decision we make. This is not just a promise but a profound transformation waiting to unfold.

Let me, Reza Abelechian, guide you through the methodologies that pave the streets of this envisioned world. Born under the Iranian sun, raised amidst the Danish winds of change, and now settled in the bustling heart of London, I have woven the tapestry of my life with the threads of business acumen and philanthropic endeavours. At the age of 42, I stand before you as a witness to the power of long-term vision in shaping societies.

Scepticism may cloud the horizon of your thoughts, whispering doubts about the practicality of such an idealistic approach. How, you might ask, can we prioritize unborn generations when current dilemmas demand immediate attention? The answer lies within these pages, where scepticism is met with tangible strategies, where doubts dissolve into the clarity of actionable wisdom.

Envision with me a political landscape where every law, every policy, and every diplomatic gesture is a step towards a verdant future. Here, you are not a passive observer; you are an integral part of the narrative, a co-creator of the world that will be the inheritance of our descendants. Through this transformative journey, you will witness the unfolding of a new paradigm in governance, one where the echoes of our actions resonate with the aspirations of those yet to walk the Earth.

This book is not merely a collection of thoughts but a commitment, a pact between us and the generations that will follow. By turning each page, you reinforce the value of foresight in our political sphere and become an architect of a legacy that transcends time.

Now, allow me to take you deeper to the heart of our exploration. Imagine a council not of today's leaders but tomorrow's beneficiaries; their voices are channelled through the wisdom of our present choices. This is not a fantasy. It is a practical framework for a sustainable political system that I will meticulously outline.

How often have you seen the natural world erupt in a symphony of life? This imagery embodies our political decisions when we plant them in the soil of foresight. Such vision can be the bedrock of nations, ensuring that prosperity is not a fleeting moment in history but a lasting era.

Do you feel the call to be part of this monumental shift? Perhaps you wonder if your voice, vote, and actions can ignite such change. Let me assure you that through the strategies laid out in this book, you will find the levers of transformation at your fingertips.

Reflect on this: What if today's policies were designed not only to solve our immediate challenges but also to sow seeds for a future we will never see? This book offers a lens to view such a future, not through the murky glass of short-term gains but with the clarity of enduring legacy.

We must tread lightly with our words. Like an artist's brush, language can colour the world with shades of possibility or cast it in the shadow of doubt. Through simple language, the complex becomes accessible, and the profound becomes tangible.

The rhythm of our discourse must mirror the pulse of life itself—dynamic, varied, and full of energy. Here, the cadence of our political aspirations will dance in harmony with future needs.

In conversations past, we've heard the echoes of great thinkers and leaders, their quotations serving as beacons through the fog of uncertainty. This book, too, will summon their wisdom, anchoring our vision in the rich soil of human experience.

To show the path ahead, we must offer more than dry explanations; we must paint with the vibrant hues of real-life stories and anecdotes that breathe life into the abstract and illuminate our principles.

Imagine Political Decisions Driven by Future Generations is not just a title; it's an invitation. An invitation to walk a new path, to craft a narrative where every political stride taken is a step towards a future that smiles back at us with gratitude.

Imagine, then, the world as a garden that we tend. Each policy is a seed, each law a nurturing gesture, and each international accord promises growth. This is the world we can cultivate together—a world that flourishes under the careful watch of our present for the boundless potential of our future.

Let this book be the start of that journey, the map that guides us toward the horizon of hope. In the imagining of such a world, we find not only inspiration but also the blueprint for a reality where the legacy of our time becomes the foundation for the ages to come.

Interpersonal Eden

Imagine Friendships Unbounded by Distance

In the tapestry of human history, connection threads have always intertwined, creating a fabric of relationships that span the globe. Yet, to truly appreciate the unbounded nature of modern friendships, we must travel back in time. Envision a world where oceans and continents divide not just lands but hearts and minds, where the mere thought of transcending such vast distances to maintain a friendship was a flight of fancy reserved for dreamers and poets.

It was during the era of great exploration, as caravels and galleons etched white trails across the blue vastness, that friendships first dared to defy distance. Letters, sealed with wax and hope, voyaged for months, carrying whispers of kinship across unfathomable miles. Through wars and revolutions, through the rise and fall of empires, these epistolary friendships survived, fueled not by frequency of contact but by the depth of words exchanged.

The Industrial Revolution brought steam power, and with it, a world shrunk by locomotives and steamships.

Telegrams clicked across continents in mere hours, a marvel that brought immediacy to remote communication. The 20th century buzzed with innovation as telephones connected voices instantly, and friendships could flourish without needing a pen, ink, or postage.

From the past to the present, the digital age has ushered in an era where geographical barriers have all but dissolved. The internet, a sprawling web of connectivity, has crafted a new paradigm for friendship. Social media, email, and instant messaging allow for real-time communication, making the world a potential gathering place for like-minded souls.

Yet why, one might ponder, does history matter now? It's simple. Understanding the journey of how friendships have evolved to transcend space informs our appreciation of the connections we forge today. It reminds us that while the tools have changed, the essence of friendship—sharing, support, and understanding—remains timeless.

As we segue into the contemporary exploration of our topic, let's pause and ask ourselves: How do we nurture friendships not limited by the miles between us? How do they grow, unfurling like sails against the horizon of our shared humanity?

Amidst the cacophony of daily life, there's a silent revolution taking place—a revolution of relationships unfettered by proximity. Within this new chapter, we delve into narratives that celebrate the endurance of long-distance friendships. Despite being separated by continents, we'll encounter individuals who have forged bonds as strong as those formed in face-to-face interactions. Their stories unfold in text messages that cross time zones, video calls that bridge the cultural chasms, and shared experiences that are enjoyed synchronously, though miles apart.

Consider the tale of Ana from Brazil and Zoe from Australia. Their friendship bloomed in the most unexpected places—an online forum for gardening enthusiasts. Language barriers wilted away amid discussions of petunias and peonies. They swapped secrets of the soil as easily as if they were neighbours leaning over a shared fence. Distance, once a formidable chasm, became a mere footnote in their flourishing friendship.

Then there's Jamal, whose business travels often take him away from home. Yet, his bond with his childhood friend, Marcus, remains unbroken. They play chess, a timeless game, now reimagined on virtual boards where their moves, though made weeks apart, keep the conversation and competition alive.

In these stories and countless others, the question arises: what is the glue that holds these friendships together? Is it the mutual respect that blooms from understanding different cultures or the shared laughter that echoes through the fibre-optic cables? Perhaps it's the realization that finding a kindred spirit is a treasure in this vast world—one not to be relinquished simply due to geographical divides.

Friendship, as it turns out, is an art. It requires the painter's brush to stroke across the canvas of our shared experiences, blending the colours of our individual lives into a masterpiece of connection. It's a symphony where the notes of our interactions create a harmony that resonates, regardless of where the music is played.

But, the challenges of maintaining such relationships persist even in this connected age. Time zones can jumble schedules, and the absence of physical presence can sometimes allow the ghost of loneliness to creep in. Yet, those who navigate these waters know that the effort is worth the reward. They understand that every message sent is like a beacon of light, cutting through the darkness of distance to say, "You are not alone."

In the following pages, we'll explore these dynamics further, examining the intricacies of friendships that thrive on the intangible yet powerful connections of the human spirit. We'll witness how love and camaraderie can be sustained and grow without the luxury of proximity.

Imagine, just for a moment, a world where every friendship has the potential to be as close as the nearest screen, as warm as the most recent message. In this world, distance is but a word, a relic of a time when the heart's reach was limited by the physical realm. Here, in the narratives of unbounded friendships, we see that no sea is too vast, no mountain too high, to keep us apart from those we hold dear.

Imagine Romantic Love Free of Fear

In the realm of the heart, the pursuit of romantic love often navigates through tumultuous seas of emotions. At its core, this journey seeks harbours of trust and freedom, untouched by the tempests of fear and insecurity. To fully engage with this exploration of love unshackled by dread, one must first grasp the essence of the crucial elements at play.

Venture into a world where the terms 'trust,' 'freedom,' 'fear,' and 'insecurity' are not just mere words but the pillars upon which the architecture of fearless love is constructed. As we voyage into the depths of relationships, these concepts shall be our guiding stars, where the waters run clear of doubt, and the winds whisper of unfettered affection.

Trust, a cornerstone of any profound connection, is the unwavering belief in the reliability, truth, and strength of one's partner. It is the soil in which the roots of a relationship grow deep, providing the nourishment for love to flourish. When trust is present, lovers can dare to be vulnerable, to expose the tender underbelly of their desires and fears, knowing they will be met with understanding rather than judgment.

Freedom in love is the liberating breeze that allows individuals to be wholly themselves within the embrace of a relationship. It is the absence of constraints, where each person is encouraged to pursue their passions and dreams, all the while intertwined with the journey of their significant other. This freedom is not about detachment; rather, it is about the choice to remain connected without the fetters of possession or control.

Fear, that insidious spectre, often creeps into the heart's chambers, casting shadows of doubt and misgiving. It is the whisper that questions the fidelity of one's partner, the spectre that turns innocent actions into perceived threats. In a love devoid of fear, partners navigate their togetherness with a sense of security, allowing no room for the baseless anxieties that can corrode the very foundation of their bond.

Insecurity, the sibling of fear, manifests as a persistent uncertainty about one's worth or the relationship's stability. It is the thief of joy, pilfering moments of happiness with thoughts of inadequacy or anticipated loss. When love transcends insecurity, partners stand on the solid ground of mutual respect and self-assurance, bolstering each other against the storms of self-doubt.

Imagine a couple strolling through a meadow, their hands entwined but their strides unimpeded by the other's pace. This image is a metaphor for the real-world concept of freedom within a relationship. Each person moves independently, yet their paths are aligned, their rhythms in sync. They are together by choice, not by necessity; their love is a dance of individuality and togetherness.

Conversely, consider the image of a lighthouse, steadfast and unyielding, casting its beam across the dark waves to guide ships safely to shore. This is trust personified—a beacon that remains constant and true, even when the night is at its darkest. It is the assurance that one is not alone, that there is someone who will always provide light in obscurity.

Now, envision a fortress, its walls high and impenetrable, designed to keep out any potential threat. This is the heart encased in fear, isolated and defended against the possibility of hurt. But in our tale, the walls crumble, for love without fear does not need such barriers. It thrives in openness, in the willingness to face vulnerability with courage.

Lastly, picture a scale perfectly balanced, with neither side outweighing the other. This represents the equilibrium of a relationship free from insecurity, where each partner holds equal value, and doubts of self-worth or jealousy do not weigh down their love.

This narrative does not just dare to dream; it weaves the very fabric of a reality where romantic love is unburdened by trepidation and self-doubt. It is a chronicle of connections that soar on the wings of assurance and autonomy, untethered by the chains of apprehension. As we delve deeper into these pages, let the words be both mirror and window—reflecting your own experiences and offering vistas into the lives of those who have found such exquisite freedom in love.

The journey is not without challenges, for the human heart is a complex vessel, often carrying the remnants of past hurts and disappointments. But in this exploration, we shall discover the beauty of love's true potential—unrestrained, bold, and gloriously fearless.

In the following chapters, tales of lovers who have traversed the path to love free of fear will unfold. They have nurtured their bond with the understanding that the most vital relationships are those where trust is given freely, where freedom is celebrated, where fear has no foothold, and where insecurity finds no refuge.

Through their stories, we will witness the transformational power of love unbound by the fetters of fright—a love that is as expansive as the universe, as radiant as the stars. Here, in the realm of fearless romance, hearts are not held captive by shadows; they are liberated, beating in harmonious tandem, singing a song of love that resonates through the ages.

Imagine Families as Sanctuaries of Support

In the quiet suburb of Green Meadows, nestled among the rolling hills and sprawling parks, a family's story speaks volumes about the transformative power of unwavering emotional support. In this tranquil setting, where children's laughter often mingles with the chirp of morning birds, we find the Harrison household—a tapestry of diverse personalities, each thread as integral as the next.

The main players in this real-life drama are the Harrisons: Michael, a dedicated father and local doctor; Emily, a compassionate mother and part-time librarian; and their three children—Sophie, Alex, and little Grace, each with their unique challenges and dreams. Together, they form a unit that embodies the essence of family as a sanctuary of support.

Sophie, the eldest at seventeen, faces the challenge of navigating the choppy waters of adolescence, with its pressure to excel academically and socially. Alex, the middle child at fourteen, grapples with the trials of being differently-abled, living with autism in a world that often misunderstands him. Grace, the youngest at eight, endeavours to carve her niche in the family, seeking attention and affirmation in the shadow of her older siblings.

The core challenge for the Harrisons was to create a home environment that could be a fortress against the external pressures that each member faced. As with any family, tensions and misunderstandings were not uncommon, but the manner in which they chose to address these issues set them apart.

Harrison's approach was not grand gestures or sweeping reforms; instead, it was a tapestry of small, consistent acts of understanding and acceptance. Michael and Emily fostered open communication, ensuring that family meetings were a safe space where each voice, however small or uncertain, was heard and valued. They implemented strategies such as individual 'listening sessions,' where attention was undivided, and empathy was the currency.

The results were heartwarming. Sophie found the confidence to share her fears about the future, which led to the family rallying around her during exam season with encouragement and practical help. Alex's unique perspective was celebrated, and his siblings learned sign language to better communicate with him, forging a deeper bond. Grace's creative flair was nurtured, and her art adorned the walls of the Harrison home, a testament to her blossoming self-esteem.

Upon reflection, these strategies were not without their flaws. There were days when patience wore thin, when misunderstandings led to raised voices rather than resolutions. Yet, the family's commitment to re-centre and learn from these moments provided invaluable lessons in resilience and forgiveness.

Visual aids like the family's communication whiteboard adorned with schedules, affirmations, and notes of appreciation served as daily reminders of their shared commitment to support one another. These tools were not mere decorations but integral parts of the sanctuary they built together.

The Harrison narrative connects to the larger concept of family as a fundamental unit of society, one that has the potential to be a bastion of emotional strength. It challenges the notion that families are just bound by blood or law, proposing instead that they are forged through the fires of shared experiences and mutual support.

As you, the reader, absorb the essence of the Harrison family's journey, ponder this: What small steps can you take to fortify your own family's bonds? How can you contribute to transforming your home into a sanctuary where every member, regardless of age or ability, feels seen, heard, and valued?

In the following pages, we will delve deeper into the heart of what makes a family not just a group of individuals living under one roof but a sanctuary of support. This refuge empowers its members to face the world with courage and grace. Join me as we explore how families like the Harrisons and perhaps your own can become the bedrock of solace and strength in an ever-changing world.

Imagine a World Where Empathy Prevails

In a world teeming with complexities and ceaseless changes, one might dare to imagine a different reality—one where the pulse of society beats with a rhythm of understanding, where the currency of interaction is not self-interest but empathy. Imagine a world where empathy prevails.

In the bustling cities and the quiet rural landscapes alike, the human condition is fraught with a myriad of challenges. The streets echo with the footsteps of individuals, each lost in their thoughts, their worries, their silent battles. From the commuter absorbed in their daily routine to the child navigating the labyrinth of social norms, there is an underlying thread of disconnect—a chasm that grows with every averted gaze and every unheard plea for help.

The crux of our societal woes lies not in the individual struggles but in the collective apathy that has seeped into the bedrock of our interactions. It manifests in the cold shoulder given to the homeless man on the corner, in the impatient honk at a faltering driver, and in the rolling eyes at a colleague's repeated story. This apathy is the antithesis of empathy, and its prevalence has profound implications.

Should this trend continue unabated, the fabric of society risks unravelling. Relationships may falter under the weight of misunderstanding, communities may fracture along lines of indifference, and social cohesion could give way to a fragmented world of isolated individuals. The consequences are dire: a society devoid of empathy is one where compassion grows scarce, and without compassion, the very essence of our humanity dims.

Yet, within this tapestry of challenges lies an opportunity—a chance to weave empathy into the very fabric of our interactions. The solution is as simple as it is profound: foster empathetic engagement at every level of society. From education systems nurturing empathy in young minds to workplaces valuing emotional intelligence, the seeds of change are ready to be sown.

How, then, do we cultivate this garden of empathy? It begins with education, teaching children not just to read and write but to listen and feel. Curriculums must include emotional literacy, helping students understand and manage their own emotions and, in turn, recognize and respond to the feelings of others.

In the workplace, empathy can be encouraged through policies that promote work-life balance, understanding that employees are not just cogs in a machine but people with lives full of complexity. Leadership training can emphasize the importance of empathy in management, creating a ripple effect that transforms organizational culture.

On a societal level, the media can play a critical role by highlighting stories of understanding and compassion, shaping public opinion, and inspiring acts of empathy. Governments can facilitate this shift by supporting initiatives that bridge divides and bring people together, whether through community-building projects or public forums for shared dialogue.

Evidence of empathy's power is not just anecdotal; it's grounded in research. Studies have shown that when individuals engage in empathetic behaviour, they experience increased levels of happiness and reduced stress. In schools where emotional literacy programs are implemented, there are marked improvements in student behaviour and academic performance. Companies that prioritize empathy often report better employee morale and higher customer satisfaction.

Of course, there are alternative routes to nurturing a more empathetic society. Some advocate for technological solutions, like virtual reality experiences that allow individuals to 'walk in someone else's shoes.' Others propose a more philosophical shift, encouraging mindfulness and self-reflection as means to cultivate internal empathy. While these methods hold merit, they complement rather than replace the need for systemic change.

In the next chapters, we will dissect these alternative solutions, evaluating their potential to contribute to an empathetic revolution. We will venture into the stories of individuals and communities that have embraced these alternatives, painting a picture of the myriad ways empathy can manifest.

Imagine, then, a world where empathy prevails, where the shared experience of being human is acknowledged and celebrated. Imagine a society where every person feels seen, understood, and valued. Through the implementation of these solutions and the cultivation of empathetic understanding, such a world is within reach. Let us take these steps together, forging a path toward a more compassionate society—one interaction, one moment of understanding at a time.

Imagine Respect as the Universal Language

In the grand tapestry of human interaction, words are the threads that weave our collective story. Yet, it is not merely the words themselves that hold the power but the intent behind them. Now, envision a reality where respect forms the cornerstone of every conversation and dignity is not an ideal but the essence of communication. Picture a world where respect is the universal language.

From the respectful nod of acknowledgement to the earnest handshake of agreement, this language transcends verbal expression, manifesting in actions, attitudes, and an unwavering commitment to honour the intrinsic worth of every individual. Such a world is not merely a utopian dream but a practical vision grounded in the potential for human decency and mutual regard.

The proposition at the heart of this vision is clear: if humanity were to embrace respect as its lingua franca, the ripple effects would transform our global landscape. The claim is bold but rooted in the belief that respect carries the seeds of peace, understanding, and progress within it.

Evidence of the transformative power of respect is found in the most foundational unit of society—the family. When family members interact with respect, they lay a foundation of trust and security. Children raised in this environment are more likely to develop into confident adults who value themselves and others. Studies in family dynamics corroborate this, showing that respect within the household correlates with lower incidences of conflict and higher levels of emotional well-being.

But what happens when this principle is extended beyond the private sphere into the public domain? Delving deeper, one finds historical precedence in societies prioritizing honour and respect. Take, for instance, the ancient codes of conduct that governed interactions among samurai in feudal Japan. The principle of respect was paramount, not only maintaining order but also fostering a culture that celebrated honour and dignity above all else.

Sceptics may counter this claim by pointing to the complexity of modern societies. They argue that respect as a universal language is impractical in a world of conflicting ideologies and interests. Furthermore, they might highlight examples where respect is either abused as a tool for subjugation or dismissed as a sign of weakness.

In response to such counter-evidence, it is crucial to clarify the definition of true respect. It is not a veneer of politeness used to mask oppressive intentions, nor is it a submissive bow to authority. Genuine respect is reciprocal; it acknowledges the humanity of the other without sacrificing one's own. It is a language spoken not only in words but in recognising each person's right to autonomy and self-expression.

Building upon this further, the concept of respect as a universal language does not negate the value of cultural diversity or individual uniqueness. On the contrary, it enhances these qualities. When respect permeates interactions, it allows for differences to be approached with curiosity rather than fear and for dialogue to replace confrontation.

The conclusion that emerges is not merely a reinforcement of the original assertion but an invitation to witness its realization. By fostering respect at every level—within families, communities, nations, and international relations—society can witness the emergence of a more compassionate and cohesive world. This vision is not devoid of challenges but promises a brighter collective future.

Imagine, then, a world where respect is the universal language. A world where every individual, regardless of background or belief, communicates from a place of inherent dignity. It is a world where the very act of interaction affirms our shared humanity. Such a world is not beyond our grasp; it awaits our collective effort to speak the language of respect—one word, one gesture and one interaction at a time.

The Altruistic Impulse

Imagine Wealth Measured in Acts of Kindness

In a world teeming with the clamour of coins and the rustle of banknotes, a concept emerges so profoundly different that it challenges the very bedrock of our understanding of wealth. Imagine a society where the currency is neither gold nor paper but rather the tangible warmth of human generosity.

To properly comprehend this notion, we must first define what is meant by 'wealth' in such an extraordinary context. Traditionally, wealth is quantified by accumulating financial assets and material possessions. In our envisioned society, however, wealth is gauged by the frequency and impact of acts of kindness. These are the selfless deeds performed without expectation of recompense, driven purely by the desire to contribute positively to the lives of others.

Expanding on the critical elements of this reimagined wealth, one must consider its forms and manifestations. It could be as simple as a shared meal with a stranger or as monumental as a shelter built by the hands of volunteers for people experiencing homelessness. Each act, regardless of size, adds to an individual's wealth.

Though a novel idea in modern times, the historical roots of measuring wealth through benevolence can be traced back to ancient philosophies and religious teachings that espoused the virtue of altruism. In these contexts, moral richness was often considered superior to material abundance.

Contextualizing within a broader framework, this concept dismantles the conventional economic systems that dominate today's world. It proposes a paradigm where social capital—the networks and relationships built on trust and mutual aid—takes precedence over financial capital.

Real-world applications of this idea are not merely flights of fancy. They can be found in small communities where barter systems thrive on the goodwill of individuals. On larger scales, they manifest in the volunteerism that underpins many non-profit organizations and social movements.

It is crucial to address common misconceptions surrounding this notion of wealth. Some may argue that it is impractical that a society cannot function on kindness alone. Yet, what is often overlooked is the transformative power that acts of kindness have on both the giver and the receiver, fostering a sense of community and shared purpose.

Could you imagine living in such a world? One where the measure of your success is the smiles you've coaxed onto faces and the burdens you've lifted from weary shoulders?

In this imagined society, the narratives that unfold on the streets tell tales of wealth beyond measure. There's the baker who, rather than discarding unsold bread, hands it to those with empty stomachs—the wealth in his heart evident in the glow of gratitude from those he feeds.

Consider the children in parks, planting trees, their laughter mingling with the rustle of leaves. Each sapling a deposit into their future wealth, growing as steadfastly as their young spirits.

Adverbs and adjectives are like the garnish on a dish—too much, and it overwhelms the palate. So, let us focus instead on the stark, unadorned truth. Kindness is the currency that never devalues, the investment that never depreciates.

The rhythm of this society is not dictated by the relentless ticking of the stock market but by the steady heartbeat of its people. Some beats are soft, almost imperceptible—the silent helping hand on a difficult day. Others are loud resonant—the collective effort to rebuild after a calamity.

"Isn't that an idealist's daydream?" a sceptic might inquire, voice laced with a tinge of cynicism. But is it not the dreamers who have shaped our most extraordinary realities?

When wealth is measured in acts of kindness, every interaction is an opportunity to enrich oneself and another. There is no poverty of the heart, for the spirit of generosity is boundless.

"Let us be kind," whispers a mural on a city wall, the words painted by anonymous hands. It serves as both a declaration and a gentle reminder of the wealth surrounding us, waiting to be acknowledged, grown, and shared.

As we turn the page on old definitions and embrace this new measure of wealth, we embark on a journey of reimagining prosperity. It's a narrative that weaves through the fabric of humanity, stitching together stories of compassion and communal triumph.

Ultimately, wealth measured in acts of kindness crafts a legacy that outlives any material inheritance. It builds bridges where walls once stood and lights a path in the darkest times. When we choose to value kindness above all, we create a genuinely immeasurable wealth.

Imagine Volunteering as a Pillar of Society

In the bustling heart of urban sprawl, where skyscrapers reach for the heavens and the cacophony of daily life drowns out the murmur of individual dreams, there lies a community centre that stands as a beacon of hope. The centre, a modest two-story building with walls adorned in vibrant murals, sits snugly between a bakery and a library, both of which often contribute to the centre's causes. This is the stage upon which our story unfolds, a tale of the resolve and compassion of ordinary people who choose to make an extraordinary difference.

At the heart of this narrative are the volunteers, a diverse tapestry of souls from all walks of life. There is Maria, a retired schoolteacher whose eyes sparkle with the wisdom of her years and whose gentle demeanour soothes the most troubled spirits. Beside her stands Jamal, a college student with dreams as tall as the skyscrapers, fueled by a passion for social justice. Their backgrounds differ as much as their ages, yet they share a common purpose: to uplift their community.

The challenge that brings them together is the centre's flagging youth program, a vital lifeline for the neighbourhood's teenagers. With dwindling funds and waning interest, the program faces the threat of closure—a devastating blow to a demographic already besieged by the lures of the street. The question looming large question is survival: how can they reinvigorate the program and secure its future?

Strategies begin to take shape through brainstorming sessions that buzz with ideas. Maria proposes leaning into the arts, offering classes that could kindle the creative flames in young hearts. On the other hand, Jamal suggests mentorship pairings, fostering bonds that could guide youths toward brighter horizons. Together, they weave a robust approach, blending education with inspiration, guidance, with expression.

The results are nothing short of miraculous. Attendance soars as word spreads of the program's revitalization. Murals begin to bloom along the centre's exterior, each a testament to a young artist's newfound confidence. College acceptance letters become a cause for celebration, with mentors standing proudly beside their protégés. The data speaks volumes: incidents of youth-related troubles in the neighbourhood plummet while graduation rates climb.

As Reza Abelechian, I reflect deeply on this success. The centre's triumph is not just in the numbers but in the stories etched upon each participant's journey. The program's revival serves as a compelling case study for the transformative power of volunteering. Yet, it's crucial to acknowledge the setbacks, the moments of doubt, and the trials that tested the resolve of our volunteers. It is within these trials that the true strength of the community centre's mission is revealed.

Visual aids punctuate the narrative, from before-and-after photos of the centre's walls to charts depicting the program's impact. These images serve not just as proof of progress but as artefacts of the community's collective spirit.

This case study, though focused on a singular instance, is a microcosm of the larger narrative that I, Reza, am championing in "Imagine." Volunteering is the bedrock upon which a society can be transformed, with each act of service acting as a stone in a much grander edifice.

And so, dear reader, I leave you with a thought to ponder: What if we found our community centre to champion? What would our world look like if, like Maria and Jamal, we all took up the mantle of service?

The streets of our cities could be corridors of colour, our neighbourhoods symphonies of support. The wealth of a community, after all, is measured not in its coffers but in the hearts of its people. When we volunteer, we don't just give our time—we share our essence, and in doing so, we enrich the world around us.

Let us imagine a society where volunteering is not just an act of charity but a cornerstone of our daily existence. Here, in the collective endeavour to lift one another, we find the truest, most accurate form of wealth—a wealth that knows no bounds and whose currency is the inexhaustible kindness of the human spirit.

As the sun dips below the horizon, casting a golden hue over the urban landscape, one can't help but feel a sense of awe at the power of collective action. The legacy of our kindness will ripple through generations, a timeless treasure that outshines the fleeting sparkle of material wealth.

Now, I ask you: Will you be the next to volunteer to take a step forward and be part of the grand tapestry of change? Will you, too, imagine?

Imagine Generosity as the Currency of Commerce

In a universe parallel to the community centre's bustling streets and altruistic hum, imagine a marketplace pulsating with a different kind of energy. Here, the currency is not minted by governments or backed by gold, but rather, it is the essence of human kindness: generosity. Imagine a world where the well-being of others is not a byproduct of business but the very heart of all economic exchange.

Can you fathom a society where every transaction begins with the question, "How can I help?" instead of "What can I get?" This is the realm we explore, where generosity is not just a virtue but the backbone of commerce.

What makes this concept so revolutionary? To understand its profundity, we must delve into the core of our current economic system and contrast it with this radical alternative. Our traditional commerce is driven by profit, a relentless pursuit of personal or shareholder gain. But in this new world, generosity guides decisions, with the prosperity of the community held in equal esteem as individual success.

How do businesses operate when generosity is their currency? They flourish by fostering relationships, by giving more than they receive, and by measuring success not in profits but in positive impacts. Consumers, in turn, support these businesses, knowing that their patronage is an investment in the greater good. The similarities in these two systems lie in their exchange structure, but the spirit behind the transaction is where we find stark differences.

Where profit-driven companies may cut corners to save costs, generosity-led businesses invest in quality and sustainability. Where traditional commerce might exploit labour, a generosity-centered economy ensures fair conditions and opportunities for personal growth. The contrast is as clear as day and night – one system takes, the other gives.

Visual aids are not needed to see the impact of such a paradigm shift. Imagine the streets lined with stores where the proprietors know your name, where products come with stories of their improved lives, and where every purchase supports a cause.

This is not mere idealism; it's a blueprint for a reimagined future. The implications of such a system are profound. It would redefine success, reshape our communities, and rebuild trust in a world often driven by self-interest. It would challenge the very foundations upon which modern capitalism stands.

But you may ask, "Is such a world possible?" Look to the community centre, where volunteers like Maria and Jamal prove that the currency of kindness is not only viable but valuable. Their generosity has transformed lives and uplifted an entire neighbourhood. If this model can thrive in a microcosm, why not in the macrocosm of global commerce?

As we ponder the real-world relevance of this concept, we begin to see glimmers of it in contemporary movements: the rise of social enterprises, the growing trend of corporate social responsibility, and the conscious consumerism that prioritizes ethical practices over cheap prices.

The echoes of this new economy are already among us. Companies that adopt fair trade practices give back a portion of their profits to community projects, prioritizing their employees' well-being – these are the harbingers of change.

And yet, the transition is not without its challenges. The inertia of old systems, the scepticism of cynics, and the fear of the unknown are formidable barriers. But as history shows, the most significant changes often start with the simplest acts.

This is no mere flight of fancy; it is a call to action.

Imagine, if you will, a world where generosity is as common in business as handshakes are today, where every exchange enriches not just the buyer and the seller but the entire fabric of society. Where commerce is a dance of mutual aid, and every participant moves to the rhythm of reciprocal benevolence.

This is the world we can create. It begins with a single act of generosity, a single business that dares to be different, a single consumer who chooses to care. It's a world where the question "What's in it for me?" becomes "What's in it for us?"

So, dear reader, as you close this chapter and step back into the reality you know, take a moment to reflect on the power of imagination. For it is within our capacity to dream that lies the seeds of the future we wish to cultivate.

Imagine then, and let that imagination guide your actions. In a world where generosity is the currency of commerce, we all become wealthier, not in coins or notes, but in the

currency that truly matters: kindness, compassion, and
community.

Imagine Education Focused on Moral Development

In a landscape where institutions are temples of knowledge and growth, imagine an education system with a heartbeat synchronized to the rhythm of moral fortitude. Picture classrooms where character formation is as crucial as the equations on the blackboard and where young minds are nurtured to become scholars and global citizens with an unwavering compass of ethics.

As we endeavour to sculpt such an educational paradigm, we embark on a journey of intellectual pursuit and character building. The goal is simple yet profound: to craft an educational experience where moral development is paramount, fostering a sense of global citizenship that transcends borders and unites hearts.

To cultivate such an environment, specific prerequisites must be in place. A robust curriculum that integrates ethical discourse, educators trained in moral philosophy, and an atmosphere that encourages critical thinking and empathy are just the beginning. Resources such as texts on moral theory, case studies on ethical dilemmas, and platforms for community engagement are the building blocks of this mission.

Imagine a blueprint for this transformative journey. At its core, it involves a sequence of phases: laying the foundation with theoretical knowledge, practising through real-world application, reflecting on personal and societal impacts, and finally, embodying these values in daily life.

Let's delve into the details, shall we? We begin by instilling the fundamental principles of ethics across various cultures and philosophies. Interactive sessions that bring these theories to life, where students debate, discuss, and dissect, are essential. Role-playing scenarios and moral quandaries presented in safe but challenging environments encourage students to apply ethical reasoning.

Here's a useful tip: Encourage learners to question, challenge the status quo, and seek out diverse perspectives. But be warned, the path of moral education is fraught with discomfort as it often challenges deeply held beliefs.

As we progress, validation of this moral education takes shape not in test scores but in the actions and decisions of the students. It's in the small acts of kindness, the courage to stand up for what's right, and the resolve to act for the greater good where we see the fruits of our labour.

Should you encounter resistance, a common hurdle, do not despair. Troubleshoot by fostering open dialogue, addressing concerns with patience, and gently guiding the sceptics towards a broader view of success, including moral integrity as a critical metric.

Now, imagine the vivid imagery of this journey: a classroom where students from all walks of life gather, their faces alight with the fire of inquiry; a playground where fairness isn't just a rule in games but a practice in interactions; a community project where the hands that build are driven by hearts that care.

Engage with me for a moment, dear reader. Can you envision a generation of leaders, innovators, and thinkers whose decisions are measured not only by their outcomes but by their ethical underpinnings?

In our pursuit of simplicity, let us not be mistaken for naivety. To foster moral development is to engage in the complex dance of human nature, where each step is deliberate, and each movement is imbued with purpose.

And so, the rhythm of our sentences mirrors the rhythm of our vision – a cadence that speaks of hope, a symphony of actions that resonate with integrity.

We may intersperse our narrative with quotations that echo the wisdom of the ages or dialogues that reveal the inner workings of the moral mind. Yet, we remain grounded, always returning to the tangible, the relatable, the real.

In a single sentence, let it be said: This is education reimagined, a crusade for character, a beacon for a brighter world.

Do not merely take my word for it; see it unfold in the stories of students who carry the torch of moral excellence into every corner of their lives. Through examples and anecdotes, we demonstrate the tangible impact of our vision.

Imagine, then, an education system not as a factory of facts but as a garden of virtue. The seeds of tomorrow's responsible citizens take root within this fertile soil. As educators, parents, and mentors, it is our solemn duty to tend to this garden, to nurture these young saplings with the water of wisdom and the sunlight of moral guidance.

The currency of this education is not grades but growth; its success is measured not in accolades but in the quiet assurance of a conscience well-formed.

This, dear reader, is not a fantasy. It is a call to arms, an invitation to join a revolution of the heart and mind. As we imagine, so shall we build – an education focused on moral development, a world enriched by ethical leaders, and a future illuminated by the light of integrity.

Imagine a Global Network of Humanitarians

In the fertile grounds of imagination, where seeds of virtue and ethics in education have taken root, another vision blossoms—one of a world united in compassion and action. Imagine a global network of humanitarians, a tapestry of individuals from diverse backgrounds; each thread is woven to alleviate suffering and foster a world of greater justice and peace.

Allow me to lead you through the annals of history to the inception of such a network. It began as a whisper, a shared notion among the benevolent that boundaries on maps should not dictate the boundaries of our empathy. This whisper grew into a dialogue, and from this dialogue, a movement was born.

Set your sights on the earliest origins, where humanitarianism took shape in the hearts of those who sought to heal and help without discrimination. In ancient civilizations, the seeds of this idea were sown in various forms—sanctuaries for the weary and destitute in Greece, the philanthropic spirit of zakat in Islamic tradition, and the Jewish practice of tzedakah, a moral obligation to do what is right and just.

As we traverse through time, imagine the milestones that marked this journey. The establishment of the Red Cross in the 19th century, the Geneva Conventions, and the formation of the United Nations and its manifold agencies—are all pivotal chapters in this ever-evolving story. With each step forward, the network expanded, its reach growing wider, its grasp on the collective conscience of humanity more secure.

Picture, if you will, images that have become icons of hope: the white canvas tents of refugee camps, the blue helmets of peacekeepers, and the emblematic logos of international charities. These symbols represent safe havens and relief in times of despair and conflict.

Delve into the cultural tapestry, and you will find variations in how humanitarianism has been embraced globally. In some cultures, it is deeply entwined with religious duty, while in others, it is driven by secular human rights principles. Yet, there is unity in this diversity—the shared conviction that we are all part of one human family.

Let us turn our gaze to the present, where modern interpretations and adaptations of humanitarianism continue to unfold. Technology has bridged distances, allowing for instantaneous communication and collaboration. Social media campaigns mobilize support for causes in real-time, and crowdfunding platforms enable direct aid from donor to beneficiary. These tools have transformed the landscape of humanitarian aid, making the global network more connected and responsive than ever before.

Can you see it? A world where every individual has the power to be a humanitarian, where the act of giving transcends transaction and becomes transformational?

But this vision is not without its shadows. Challenges and controversies have emerged, questioning the motives and methods of humanitarian action. Debates over the politicization of aid, the principles of neutrality and impartiality, and the spectre of 'voluntourism' have sparked introspection within the network. Pivotal turning points, like the increasing emphasis on sustainability and local empowerment, signify a maturing understanding of what it means to help effectively.

Consider this: How do we navigate the complex ethics of intervention without imposing, exacerbating dependencies, or diluting the agency of those we aim to assist?

The answers may begin to take shape in the silence that follows such questions. The resolve to listen more than we speak, to empower rather than impose, and to collaborate rather than control are the signposts guiding the network's evolution.

Imagine the singular narrative of a life transformed by this global network—a child educated, a wound healed, a community rebuilt. In these stories, the abstract becomes concrete, and the distant becomes personal.

This global network of humanitarians is not an abstract concept nor an unreachable ideal. It is the embodiment of our collective potential for compassion and the manifestation of our innate desire to alleviate suffering. It is the realization that, in the act of helping others, we define the very essence of what it means to be human.

Each sentence and word in this narrative is a brick in the edifice of our shared humanity. Through the rhythm of our actions and the cadence of our compassion, we build a world that reflects our highest ideals.

Imagine a global network of humanitarians not as a lofty dream but as a tangible reality—a network stretching across continents, binding us together in the common pursuit of a better tomorrow.

As we imagine, so shall we build—a world enriched by the spirit of humanitarianism, a tapestry of compassion woven by the hands of countless unsung heroes, and a future illuminated by the light of hope and human dignity favour.

Imagine a World Without Fear

Imagine a world unshackled by the icy grip of fear. Can you picture it? Streets brimming with the symphony of laughter, eyes sparkling with the glint of dreams undimmed by the shadow of dread. In this realm, courage is not the absence of fear but the transcendence of it.

Imagine the artist, palette in hand, who paints not what the market wishes but what her heart screams to express. Her strokes are bold; colours clash and harmonize in a dance of rebellion against the canvas of expectations. She is not fettered by the fear of rejection, for in this world, art breathes the air of freedom, and creativity knows no bounds.

Picture the entrepreneur, whose ideas once quivered on the edge of oblivion, teetering close to the abyss of 'what if.' Now, they stand tall, unencumbered by the spectre of failure. The marketplace is a mosaic of innovation, each failure a stepping stone, each risk a badge of honour. The fear of bankruptcy is, but a distant memory, and the currency of this new world is resilience.

Envision the child in the classroom; hand raised high like a beacon. There is no fear of ridicule, no anxiety over the 'wrong' answer. Questions bubble forth, a spring of curiosity unsealed. Here, mistakes are not marks of shame but bridges to understanding, and learning is a journey of joyous discovery rather than a path of trepidation.

Now, step into the shoes of the adventurer, setting sail to uncharted territories. The horizon stretches into infinity, a challenge to the limits of the known. The fear of the unknown is a relic, a tale of old to be recounted with a smile. The thrill of exploration pulses in the veins of society, and the map of the world is a living testament to the undying spirit of adventure.

Pause for a moment. Feel your heart in this world without fear. It beats to the rhythm of possibility, each thump echoing the footsteps of those who walk the streets with heads held high, not in arrogance, but in the dignity of self-belief.

What, then, of love? Ah, love in a world without fear glows fervently, a flame unthreatened by gusts of doubt. Hearts connect, not in the safety of guarded vulnerability   but in the raw, beautiful messiness of openness. The fear of heartbreak does not loom over relationships; instead, trust is the foundation upon which bonds are forged.

But let us delve deeper. Consider the public speaker, once paralyzed by the sea of expectant faces. Now, words flow freely, a cascade of genuine expression. Audiences are no longer judges but fellow travellers on the odyssey of ideas. The dread of public humiliation has dissipated like mist under the morning sun, and in its place, a bridge of understanding is built, word by word.

Do you see it? The impact of a world where fear has lost its dominion is not a subtle shift but a transformation that reverberates through every facet of life. It is a world where potential is not caged but unleashed, where the human spirit soars on the wings of audacity.

In such a world, leadership is redefined. Leaders are not those who instil fear to command obedience but those who inspire by example, who lead from within the ranks of the hopeful. Their power lies not in their ability to intimidate but in their capacity to empower.

It is a world where the collective future is not a grim forecast of woes but a canvas of opportunity. The absence of fear is the mother of invention, fostering groundbreaking discoveries that spring from the well of unimpeded curiosity.

Would you recognize yourself in this world? Without the chains of fear, who could you become? What dreams would you chase down the alleys of reality, and what monuments of achievement could you erect in the vast landscape of human endeavour?

Challenge your fears. Dare to imagine. For in the imagining, we begin the first steps toward creation. This is the essence of our chapter—this is the heart of our story.

Imagine a world without fear—then open your eyes, and let's build it together.

The Art of Mindful Consumption

Imagine Conscious Consumption as a Path to Fulfillment

In a world where the relentless pursuit of more is often seen as the road to happiness, pause for a moment. Close your eyes. Now, imagine a different path—conscious consumption as a gateway to a more fulfilled life.

What does conscious consumption mean? Envision a scenario where every purchase is questioned, not with cynicism, but with curiosity. What is the story behind this product? Who made it? What resources were used, and can they be renewed? The idea isn't merely to consume less but to consume with intention, with awareness of the impact our choices have on the world around us.

Imagine, for instance, stepping into a clothing store. Racks teem with vibrant colours and alluring designs. Your fingers brush against the fabric, feeling the texture. But this time, instead of grabbing the first eye-catching item, you pause. You reflect on whether this garment is something you need or merely a fleeting desire. You consider the materials, the craftsmanship, and the life of the person who sewed the seams. Suddenly, the clothes are more than just objects. They are stories; they are lives; they are a part of a larger, interconnected world.

Now, think of the last meal you ate. Was it hastily purchased, a mere transaction of convenience? Imagine, instead, a meal that is a tapestry of connection. Vegetables grown by farmers who nurture their soil, bread from grains milled close to home, a piece of fruit from a tree that might as well be a neighbour. Each bite is a celebration, a communion with the environment and the community that sustains you.

What if our relationships echoed this practice of conscious consumption? Picture nurturing connections that are not based on what someone can give you materially but on mutual respect, support, and genuine interaction. Imagine friendships that flourish not from transactions or gifts but from shared experiences and heartfelt conversations.

Consider for a moment the objects in your home. Each one holds a memory, a purpose. Some might be heirlooms heavy with history and sentiment. Others might be hand-picked treasures that caught your eye at a local market, chosen not for their price tags but for their ability to spark joy every time you see them. This is not a home cluttered with impulse buys; it's a sanctuary filled with mindful selections that truly mean something to you.

Have you ever asked yourself, "Do I own my possessions, or do they own me?" A daunting question, isn't it? But within it lies the key to conscious consumption. It's about owning less and experiencing more, about finding richness in simplicity. It's about making space—not just in your physical surroundings, but in your mind and your heart—for the truly important things.

"Is this essential?" you might ask yourself the next time you're tempted by an advertisement or a sale. This simple question has the power to transform your interactions with the material world. It's an invitation to step off the treadmill of accumulation and to start walking a path of purposeful engagement.

Imagine the freedom that comes with this shift in perspective. Freed from the weight of excess, you find yourself lighter and more agile to pivot towards the experiences that truly matter. You travel not to escape life but to ensure that life doesn't escape you. You learn, you explore, you grow—not because you own a lot, but because you are mindful of what you have.

Imagine, too, the ripple effect of your conscious choices. Each decision to consume with purpose sends a message to producers, to retailers, to fellow consumers. It's a declaration that the quality of life is not measured by quantity but by the depth of our engagements with the world.

Now, let's bring this journey of imagination to a close with a question, one that is direct and perhaps a little unsettling. "What would happen if we all embraced conscious consumption?" The answer is not for me to tell but for us to find out together, one mindful choice at a time.

For in this vision of conscious consumption lies not just a path to personal fulfilment but the promise of a transformed world. It's a world where every action is an act of stewardship, every purchase a testament to our values, and every interaction a step towards a more sustainable, more connected, and more fulfilling way of life.

Imagine that.

Imagine Nurturing Relationships Beyond Material Good

Imagine, then, the potential for nurturing relationships that transcend the boundaries of material possession. Picture a life in which the connections we cherish are not defined by what we can buy for each other but by the moments we share and the mutual growth we foster.

Imagine a friendship where the currency is not gifts but laughter, empathy, and support. What would such a friendship look like? It would be one where joy comes not from the exchange of commodities but from the exchange of stories, the sharing of dreams, and the comforting presence during times of struggle. How would it feel to know that you are valued for who you are, not for what you own or what you can offer in material terms?

How often do we measure the strength of a relationship by the weight of the presents we receive instead of the weight of the love and care that is present? Can you recall a time when a simple walk with a friend, immersed in the beauty of nature and each other's company, felt more fulfilling than any expensive outing?

Consider the family ties that bind us. These bonds often become entangled with expectations of financial support or lavish gestures. But what if we stripped away these material layers? What if we found strength in the vulnerability of open conversations, in shared meals prepared with love, in the silent understanding that comes from years of shared experiences?

What if our romantic entanglements were not judged by the size of a diamond or the grandeur of a holiday but by the depth of understanding and the commitment to face life's challenges together? Imagine a love that is not showcased with ostentatious displays but is quietly affirmed through daily acts of kindness, patience and perseverance.

Pause now and think. When was the last time a relationship deepened, not because of a material gift but because of time spent together? Maybe it was a conversation that stretched into the early hours, where secrets and fears were shared. Perhaps it was standing side by side, facing adversity, finding that your bond grew stronger in the face of challenge.

Reflect on the richness that comes from relationships built on a foundation of shared values and beliefs. These are the ties that endure when the allure of materialism fades. They are the connections that thrive in simplicity, where the joy comes from mutual respect and admiration.

Have you considered the act of giving not as a transaction but as an expression of understanding and compassion? A gesture that says, "I see you, I hear you, I am with you," without the need for anything physical in return.

Imagine a community where success is not measured by accumulation but by contribution. Envision a society that values the wisdom of its elders, the energy of its youth, and the dedication of its caregivers—where the measure of one's worth is not tied to financial prosperity but to the richness of their character.

How can we foster such relationships and communities? It begins with a choice, a conscious decision to value presence over presents, to prioritize experiences over possessions. It's a commitment to listen deeply, to give freely of ourselves, and to celebrate the intangible threads that weave the tapestry of human connection.

What would happen if we started to redefine wealth, not in terms of bank accounts but in terms of our social and emotional riches? Imagine a world where the most treasured inheritance we could leave behind is the love we've shared and the lives we've touched.

Now, consider the art of conversation. Remember a dialogue that made you feel truly heard and understood. How did it compare to the fleeting satisfaction of a new purchase? There is an art to conversing that, when mastered, can lead to a more profound connection than any physical gift could ever forge.

In this envisioned future, the phrase "I'm here for you" holds more power than any material symbol of affection. It's a commitment that stands firm in the face of life's inevitable storms, a beacon of constancy and assurance.

Imagine the next generation observing our choices and the way we build and maintain our relationships. What lessons would they learn if they saw us valuing time and attention over gadgets and trinkets? How might this shape their understanding of what it means to care for someone?

As this journey through imagination draws to a close, let's not end with a question but with an invitation. Consider this a call to action to live out the principles of nurturing relationships beyond material goods. It's an invitation to invest in the wealth of connection, cherish the abundance of shared humanity, and find fulfilment in the simple yet profound act of being there for one another.

Imagine that.

Imagine Sustainable Choices for a Balanced Lifestyle

In our quest for a balanced lifestyle, sustainability is a thread that weaves through every choice we make. Picture a day starting not with the jarring sound of an alarm but with the gentle rays of the sunrise nudging you awake. Your morning ritual doesn't involve a single-use coffee pod but rather a cup of fair-trade coffee, its rich aroma mingling with the quiet of the dawn.

Have you ever pondered the impact of your daily routines on the planet? Think about the water that cascades from your showerhead. Is it a resource you cherish, or do you let it run, unappreciated, down the drain? Consider the power of a shorter shower or a water-saving nozzle and the satisfaction of conserving life's most precious resource.

When you choose what to wear, do you reach for the fast fashion, quickly bought and just as quickly discarded? Or do you select garments crafted to last, their fibres telling a story of ethical production and mindful consumption? Imagine a wardrobe curated not for quantity but for quality, where each piece is treasured and worn with pride.

A balanced lifestyle extends to what we eat. Envision a plate not piled high with processed fare, but adorned with vibrant produce, locally sourced and bursting with flavour. The act of eating becomes an experience, a moment of connection with the earth and its bounty. Can you taste the difference when your food is not just consumed but savoured when each bite is an ode to the farmers' toil and the soil's yield?

Transportation, too, is a realm ripe for sustainable choices. What if, instead of the solitary confinement of a car, you embraced the camaraderie of public transit? Perhaps you feel the wind in your hair as you cycle, your muscles powering you forward, the city's heartbeat syncing with your own. Isn't there an undeniable joy in the freedom that comes from reducing your carbon footprint?

But sustainability is not just about what you consume; it's about what you refuse. Picture a life with less clutter, where possessions don't overflow from drawers and shelves. Have you experienced the liberation that comes from letting go, from finding value not in objects but in space, in the absence of excess?

Think about the power that resides in the palm of your hand—the smartphone. How often do we replace these gadgets, chasing the latest model without a thought for the old? Now, envision a different approach: one where you hold on to devices until they no longer serve their purpose, where electronic waste is not the norm but the exception.

In the realm of work, imagine a career path that aligns with your values, where success is not quantified by profit but qualified by the positive change you create. It's a vision of professional life where burnout is not worn as a badge of honour but is actively avoided through balance and mindfulness.

Your home, too, can be a sanctuary of sustainability. Solar panels glisten on the roof, capturing the sun's energy to power your abode. Walls insulated with care keep the heat in during winter's chill and out during summer's blaze. Can you feel the comfort that comes from living in harmony with the environment, from knowing that your shelter treads lightly on the earth?

Imagine the shared spaces of our communities, the parks, and plazas where life unfolds. What if these were designed with nature in mind, buzzing with pollinators and flush with greenery? These are the lungs of our cities, spaces where we can breathe deeply and find respite from the concrete and steel.

Engage with me now in a thought experiment. What if every gift you gave was an experience rather than an item? A concert, a class, a shared adventure—these are offerings that don't collect dust but collect memories. How much more meaningful could our celebrations be if they were about time spent together rather than things given and received?

And what about the unseen choices, the ones that ripple beneath the surface of our awareness? The bank you choose, the pension plan you invest in, the companies you support—each of these decisions shapes the world we live in. Imagine aligning your financial actions with your deepest convictions, becoming an investor in a future that is equitable and green.

As the sun sets on this day of imagination, reflect on the power of your choices. Each one, no matter how small, is a step towards a balanced lifestyle, a gesture of commitment to a more sustainable world. It's the cumulation of these choices, made day after day that can transform our reality.

In this vision of tomorrow, sustainability is not a sacrifice but a source of fulfilment. It's a path paved with intention, leading to a destination of balance and harmony. Imagine, if you will, a life where every action is a reflection of your deepest values, where the mundane becomes meaningful, and every day is extraordinary.

Imagine that.

Imagine Finding Harmony Through Minimalism

Imagine a life unencumbered by the needless many, where the few bring not just function but meaning. In a world saturated with possessions, what would it feel like to strip away the superfluous until only the essential remains? Picture your living space: is it a haven of tranquillity or a cluttered maze of things seldom used and rarely appreciated?

Minimalism is not merely about having less; it's about making room for more—more energy, more clarity, more time. It's about finding harmony in simplicity. Have you ever paused to consider the weight of the possessions you carry through life? Not just the physical burden, but the mental load they impose?

Now, envision a dwelling defined by space and light, where every object earns its place not just by utility but by the joy it brings. Do your belongings serve you, or do you serve them? Picture a morning void of the frantic search for misplaced items, where every moment is your own, and serenity is the default.

Could it be that in the subtraction of things, we multiply our happiness? Delve into the heart of your home. The kitchen, often the nucleus of clutter, can transform into a model of minimalist efficiency. What if, instead of sifting through a sea of gadgets, each culinary tool was chosen thoughtfully, its presence in your space a testament to its value and versatility?

Imagine drawers that glide open to reveal a curated selection of utensils that fit neatly into your life. Can you hear the soft click of a cabinet, the gentle hum of a minimalist kitchen where every dish prepared is an exercise in focused pleasure, each ingredient honoured in the creation of a meal?

What about the clothes that swaddle you, the fabrics that embrace your skin? Imagine a closet where every article of clothing is selected with intention, a capsule wardrobe that reflects not only your style but your ethos. Each piece is not just worn but cherished. How liberating it is to dress with ease, knowing that every garment has a purpose and a story?

Let's wander through the corridors of the mind. Minimalism goes beyond the tangible; it permeates our thoughts and actions. Are your days filled with needless noise, a cacophony of tasks that scream for attention but yield little satisfaction? What if your to-do list was pruned to its most vital elements, allowing you to invest in activities that truly resonate with your soul?

Have you considered the beauty of a single flower and how it can captivate more than a whole bouquet? Apply this principle to your pursuits. Imagine spending your hours on passions that ignite your spirit, where each hobby is not just a pastime but a pathway to self-discovery and joy.

Picture the technology that pervades our lives. Screens flicker with endless notifications, demanding our gaze and fragmenting our focus. What if your digital world was a reflection of minimalist principles? A space where every app serves a distinct purpose, where your online presence is thoughtful and deliberate.

What would it mean to engage with social media not out of habit but with intention, to choose connections that uplift rather than distract? Imagine a virtual environment that mirrors the calm of your physical space, where silence is not a void but a canvas for your thoughts to flourish.

As you pare down your belongings, consider the impact on your relationships. With less to clean, maintain, and worry about, could there be more room for loved ones? Imagine interactions that are not rushed or distracted but fully present. How might your connections deepen when the excess fades away, leaving space for authentic engagement?

Turn your gaze to your work environment. Imagine a desk unburdened by clutter, where each item is purposeful, and your workflow is unimpeded by chaos. What if every task was approached with a minimalist mindset, where quality trumps quantity, and every effort is infused with care and attention?

Envision the liberation that comes with a minimalist approach to consumption. How empowering it is to resist the siren call of advertisements, to break free from the cycle of buy-and-discard. Can you feel the relief of knowing that what you own is enough, that your worth is not measured by your possessions but by the richness of your experiences?

Imagine the cumulative effect of these minimalist choices, how they ripple outward, influencing every facet of your existence. It's a journey towards less, but in this reduction, we find a surplus of life's true treasures. Here, in the embrace of minimalism, we discover not deprivation but abundance.

Imagine, if you will, a life where every decision, every acquisition, every moment is infused with intention. It's a world where the extraneous is stripped away, revealing the pure essence of joy, connection, and peace. Here, in the uncluttered expanse of the minimalist philosophy, we find harmony.

Imagine that.

Imagine Kindness Extended Through Ethical Consumerism

In a world where every dollar spent is a statement of value, imagine if kindness could extend through the very act of consumption. What if each purchase made was a seed sown into the soil of global well-being? In this chapter, we delve into the heart of ethical consumerism and explore how our everyday choices can become acts of profound kindness.

Ponder for a moment the clothes that drape your body. Each thread woven into the fabric of your attire tells a story—a narrative that spans continents and lives. What if, instead of mindlessly grabbing the latest fashion off the rack, you paused to consider the hands that crafted it? Can you visualize the faces of the workers, their hopes and struggles, as they assemble the garments that colour your world?

Now, imagine choosing to invest in a garment that carries the label of fair trade. Picture the ripple effect as your purchase ensures fair wages, dignified working conditions, and a brighter future for a community. Isn't there an undeniable warmth in the thought that the clothes hugging your skin are steeped in the essence of fairness and compassion?

Let's turn our attention to the food that graces our tables. The journey from farm to fork is often obscured, a hidden odyssey that escapes our thoughts as we savour each bite. But what if we peeled back the layers, tracing the origins of our meal? Envision the sun-drenched fields, the hands that toil, and the journey that each ingredient undertakes to nourish your body.

Imagine the impact of choosing locally sourced produce and how it supports the farmers just a stone's throw away from your kitchen window. Can you taste the difference when food is not just consumed but cherished for its local roots and the care that brought it to your plate?

But it's not just the tangible products that offer an opportunity for kindness through ethical consumerism. Consider the services that punctuate our lives—the bank where we save our money, the energy that powers our homes, the insurance that gives us peace of mind. What if these, too, were chosen with an eye towards ethics and kindness?

Picture a financial institution that invests in community development or a green energy provider that harnesses the power of the wind and sun. Imagine an insurance company that goes beyond profit, extending its reach to support vital social causes. With each decision, you cast a vote for the kind of world you wish to live in.

Now, reflect on the gadgets and devices that fill our modern existence. Technology, a beacon of progress, also casts a shadow of environmental strain and ethical dilemmas. What if your phone, your laptop, and your myriad of electronic companions were selected with an awareness of their lifecycle and the resources they consume?

Imagine a world where electronics are designed for longevity and repairability, where recycling isn't an afterthought but a fundamental aspect of the product's design. Think of the satisfaction that comes from knowing your device doesn't contribute to the growing heaps of e-waste but instead sustains a cycle of responsible use and reuse.

As we wield the power of our wallets, let us not forget the allure of experiences over possessions. How often do we squander our resources on items that quickly lose their luster when we could instead invest in moments that build memories? Picture the joy of a cooking class that not only spices up your culinary skills but also supports a local chef or a vacation that immerses you in the culture of the place without exploiting it.

In every facet of our lives, we have the choice to extend kindness through ethical consumerism. It's a path that demands mindfulness and a willingness to question the status quo. But isn't the effort worthwhile when each purchase becomes a testament to our shared humanity and the planet we call home?

What would it mean for your life if every object you owned, every service you used, every experience you indulged in was a reflection of your deepest values? How might your heart swell with the knowledge that your daily choices contribute to a kinder, more equitable world?

Imagine that.

Embracing Nature's Wisdom

Imagine Finding Harmony in Natural Ecosystems

In the hush of dawn, a solitary bird sang. Its melody wove through the crisp morning air, a natural symphony accompanied by the rustle of leaves and the gentle murmur of a nearby stream. The forest was waking, and with each passing moment, the chorus of life grew stronger. Here, in the heart of nature's embrace, one could not help but feel the pulse of the earth, the interconnected dance of existence that whispered of a harmony long forgotten.

Have you ever stood where the horizon kisses the ocean and felt your troubles ebb away with the receding tide? Or have you wandered through the woods, the scent of pine and earth grounding you as if the very soil beneath your feet could replenish your soul? These are the moments when we touch something profound, a universal truth that nature hums beneath its breath: everything is connected.

The forest, a sprawling canvas of green, bursts with life that is both seen and unseen. Each creature, from the industrious ant to the majestic eagle, plays a role in this intricate web. The trees, ancient and wise, stand as sentinels of time, their roots delving deep into the earth, drawing sustenance from the hidden springs of life.

A leaf falls, pirouetting gracefully to the ground. Could it be just a leaf, or is it a symbol of nature's eternal cycle of growth and decay, a reminder that even in death, there is beauty, and there is a purpose? It decomposes, becoming one with the soil, and from it, new life will arise. A testament to the resilience and adaptability of the natural world.

How often do we pause to consider the soil beneath our feet? This dark, rich tapestry is woven from the remnants of life, a foundation for new growth. It teems with organisms, each playing their part in breaking down matter, transforming it into nutrients, the very building blocks of life. It's a silent, unassuming process, yet without it, the splendour of the forest could not persist.

Imagine a stream, its waters clear and cool, winding through the forest like a ribbon of life. Notice the pebbles beneath the surface, each smoothed over countless years by the gentle caress of flowing water. Fish dart between the shadows, scales glinting like fragments of starlight. The stream is more than a body of water; it is a vein of the ecosystem, carrying lifeblood to all it touches.

But what of harmony? Is it merely a concept, or is it something we can truly achieve within these natural ecosystems? To find harmony, one must first understand balance. A predator culls the weak, ensuring the health of the herd. Plants convert sunlight into energy, a gift of life for those who consume them. Even the decay of the forest floor fuels the circle of life, proving that every end is but a beginning in another form.

Yet, we humans often struggle with this balance. We take more than we need, disrupting the delicate equilibrium that has existed for aeons. But imagine if we could learn from the forest, from the stream, from the soil. Imagine if we could find that same harmony within ourselves, a way to live that enriches rather than depletes.

Could it be that our own well-being is inextricably linked to the health of our natural surroundings? When the air is clean, do we not breathe more deeply? When the water is pure, do we not drink more freely? And when the land is vibrant and alive, do we not find nourishment for our bodies and our spirits?

Consider this: the choices we make ripple through the ecosystem, much like stones cast into a pond. The consequences of our actions, good or bad, spread far beyond our immediate sight. So, what if we choose to tread lightly, to act with intention and care? The ripple effect of such a choice could be the genesis of a new harmony, not just for us but for the myriad forms of life that share this planet.

The natural world thrives on interdependence. The bee pollinates the flower, which in turn provides sustenance for the bird. And so, a question arises. How can we, as intelligent beings, contribute to this dance of interdependence? Must we always take, or can we also give back, become stewards of this earth that has given us so much?

Let us imagine a world where humanity's footprint is gentle, where we emulate the cycles of the forest, the balance of the stream, and the nurturing essence of the soil. It is not beyond our reach. Small actions, when multiplied by millions, can lead to monumental change. Planting a tree, conserving water, reducing waste – these are but the first notes of a harmonious melody we can all help compose.

In the end, finding harmony in natural ecosystems is about respect – respect for the delicate intricacies of nature, for the roles each species plays, and for the very planet that sustains us. It is about recognizing that we are part of something greater than ourselves, a vast and beautiful tapestry of life.

So, as the sun sets and casts the forest in a golden glow, let us reflect on the beauty that surrounds us and on the harmony we wish to see in the world. In imagining it, we take the first step towards making it a reality. And in the stillness of the twilight, listen – perhaps you too can hear the earth's song, inviting you to join in its timeless chorus.

Imagine Resilience Through Biodiversity Conservation

Imagine the delicate dance of a butterfly as it flutters from flower to flower, its wings a kaleidoscope of vibrant colours. Each beat, a tiny miracle of nature, is a testament to the diversity that enriches our planet. This butterfly, along with countless other species, forms a mosaic of life that is not only breathtaking to behold but also crucial for the health of our ecosystems.

Have you ever pondered the resilience of life in the face of adversity? It is a resilience born from the richness of biodiversity. A single species may falter, but the web of life, with its myriad strands, holds strong. The resilience of an ecosystem is akin to a tapestry. If one thread unravels, the impact may be small, but if multiple threads loosen, the entire structure is at risk. Could it be that our survival hinges on this complex, delicate weave?

Let's delve into the realm of biodiversity conservation. Imagine a world where each of us is an active participant in safeguarding the variety of life on Earth. What if we were to cultivate an awareness that fostered respect for all living things, understanding that every organism has a role to play?

Picture a future where the jagged peaks of mountains are home to eagles that soar high above the tree line, their sharp eyes scanning the landscape below. The mountain streams team with life, from the microscopic algae to the sleek trout that navigate the currents. These high-altitude ecosystems are reservoirs of biodiversity, harbouring species that have adapted to the thin air and cold temperatures. What if these peaks, often seen as remote and untouchable, were recognized as vital organs of our planet, pumping life into the valleys below?

Let's consider the oceans, those vast, mysterious bodies of water that cradle the Earth. Here, life abounds in forms so diverse and numerous that many remain unknown to us. The ocean's depths teem with creatures that defy imagination, adapted to darkness and pressure that would crush us instantly. Is it not a marvel that such resilience exists in the face of such harsh conditions?

But why should we concern ourselves with creatures we may never see in places we may never visit? The question is as deep and fathomable as the depths of the sea itself. Reflect on this: the air you breathe, the food you consume, the stability of the climate you rely on—all are gifts from biodiversity. When we protect the diverse forms of life, we sustain the systems that support us.

Imagine forests standing tall and unbroken, where the howl of the wolf is still heard. These ancient woodlands are more than just groups of trees; they are communities pulsing with life and energy. Could we be guardians of these places, ensuring that they remain for generations to come?

Visualize a small child in a city, their hands digging into the soil of a community garden. Here, amidst the buzz of traffic, a patch of green thrives. Even in urban landscapes, biodiversity can be nurtured. City parks, green roofs, and gardens can become havens for insects, birds, and small mammals. Small pockets of nature, perhaps, but with the power to connect us to the larger world beyond our concrete confines.

But how does one instil a sense of stewardship in the human heart? Education is a key. By teaching our children about the wonder of life in all its forms, we can ignite a passion for conservation that burns brighter with each passing year. Can you envision schools where children learn not just from books but from the whispering grasses and the wise old trees?

Imagine policies that prioritize the protection of habitats, where governments and corporations work hand in hand with environmentalists. What if sustainable practices became the norm, not the exception? Could economies thrive by honouring the planet rather than exploiting it?

Each choice we make leaves a mark upon the Earth. What if we chose to consume less, to reduce our footprint, and to live in a way that acknowledges our place in the natural order? Making a difference might seem daunting, but remember, even the mightiest river starts as a mere trickle.

Pause and listen to the rhythm of the Earth. It beats in the wings of the butterfly, in the heart of the forest, in the ebb and flow of the tides. This rhythm is a call to action—a plea for mindfulness and care. Will we answer?

It is time to imagine a world where resilience through biodiversity conservation is not just a dream but a reality. Our actions can be the seeds of change, sprouting hope for a future where all life thrives. So, let us plant those seeds, tend to them, and watch as our collective garden grows into a legacy of balance and beauty—a world where imagination and resilience go hand in hand.

Imagine Serenity in the Wilderness

As the dawn's early light creeps over the horizon, it bathes the wilderness in a gentle glow; the world awakens in a symphony of sounds. Have you ever found yourself standing at the edge of a vast forest, the air alive with the chirping of birds and the rustle of leaves? It's in these hushed moments of the morning that the wilderness speaks to those who listen.

Imagine the serene beauty of an untouched landscape, where the only paths are those etched by the hooves of deer and the padded feet of foxes. Picture the towering pines and ancient oaks standing as silent sentinels, their branches swaying in a dance as old as the Earth itself. What secrets do they whisper to the wind? What stories could they tell if we only knew how to hear?

In the heart of the wilderness, a river runs—a silvery thread weaving through the mosaic of greens and browns. Its waters, cool and clear, cascade over smooth stones and fallen logs, the constant rush a testament to the never-ending journey of nature. Have you ever traced the course of a river, following its bends and curves, marvelling at how it carves its way through the land? There is a lesson in its relentless flow—the teaching of persistence and the power of gradual change.

Consider the delicate beauty of a wildflower meadow, a riot of colours that waves in the breeze. Each petal, each leaf, is a masterpiece of design, perfected by the hands of time. Amidst this splendour, butterflies dance, and bees hum, each creature playing its part in an intricate ballet of life. Could such simplicity hold the key to the joy we so often seek?

In the quiet of the wilderness, one might stumble upon a secluded pond, its surface a mirror reflecting the sky above. Frogs croak from lily pads, and dragonflies dart with jewel-like brilliance. Have you ever gazed into the depths of a pond, pondering what mysteries lie beneath? Each ripple on the water's surface tells a story of movement and life, yet beneath, in the stillness, there is a world unseen.

Pause for a moment and consider the wolves that roam the forests, their howls a haunting melody in the twilight hours. There is a wildness in their eyes—a reminder of what it means to be free. What lessons can we learn from these creatures, who live not by our rules but by the laws of nature? In the wolf's song, there is a call to remember our primal connection to the Earth, to embrace a spirit of adventure and untamed beauty.

Imagine the mountains, their peaks reaching for the heavens, their slopes blanketed with snow. Have you ever stood atop a mountain, the world unfurled below you, feeling both insignificant and omnipotent at once? The air is crisp, the silence profound. Here, one can truly understand solitude—not as loneliness but as a space for reflection and growth.

But amidst the serenity, a question arises—how do we protect these wild places? The wilderness is not just a refuge for the soul but a vital part of our planet's health. It is a haven for biodiversity, a reservoir of clean air and water, and a stronghold against the encroachment of civilization. What if we recognized the intrinsic value of the wild, not just for what it offers us, but for itself?

Envision a world where conservation is not a chore but a calling, where we recognize the interconnectedness of all life. The choices we make ripple across the land like the waves of a pond. Will we tread lightly, leaving no trace, or will we carve deep scars upon the face of nature?

The serenity found in the wilderness is a gift—one that demands our respect and stewardship. Can we rise to the challenge, embracing a future where the wild remains untouched, a sanctuary for all species, including our own? Imagine a legacy of conservation, a world where we walk hand in hand with nature, not as conquerors but as humble guests.

Let us hold this image in our minds: the wilderness, pristine and peaceful, a canvas of natural beauty. It is there, in the quiet places, that we find clarity. It is there that we remember what it means to be a part of something greater than ourselves. And it is there that we discover serenity, a serenity that whispers of the wild, calling us back to our roots, back to the embrace of the Earth.

So, take a moment to close your eyes and imagine— imagine serenity in the wilderness. It is more than a place; it is a state of being, a harmony with the world that sustains us. Will you answer the call?

Imagine Cultivating Kindness Towards the Environment

Gaze upon the bustling cityscape, a stark contrast to the tranquil wilderness we've just envisioned. It's a realm of concrete and steel, where nature seems to have been pushed to the margins, relegated to parks and planters. Yet, even here, in the heart of urbanity, can you imagine infusing kindness into every street, every building, every corner?

Imagine a city where green roofs sprawl across skyscrapers, where the buzzing of bees in rooftop gardens is as commonplace as the hum of traffic below. Envision communities coming together to transform vacant lots into vibrant community gardens bursting with vegetables and flowers that provide sustenance and beauty. Could this be the seed of change sown in the soil of collective effort?

Picture a world where every child learns the value of a tree, not merely for the shade it offers but for the life it sustains. Schools with outdoor classrooms, where lessons are breathed in with fresh air, rooted in the reality of the living world. What if education extended beyond the walls of schools into the realms of forests and streams, developing a sense of stewardship from the earliest age?

In the veins of the city, imagine streams and rivers once buried now daylighted, allowed to see the sun once more. Their waters, once hidden, now meander through neighbourhoods, a reminder of nature's resilience. Could we learn to value these waterways not as mere conduits for our convenience but as arteries of life, essential to the well-being of our communities?

Consider the power of a single act of kindness towards the Earth—choosing to walk or cycle instead of driving, reducing waste, or supporting local farmers. Each choice is a thread in the tapestry of conservation, a statement of care and respect for the planet. How might these simple acts, multiplied by millions, weave a new narrative for the future?

Imagine enterprises that thrive not on exploitation but on harmony with the environment. Businesses that measure success not solely by profit but by the positive impact they have on the world. What innovations could spring from such a philosophy, what solutions to the challenges we face?

Pause here. Reflect on the energy systems that power our lives. Picture a landscape where wind turbines turn gracefully in the breeze, where solar panels capture the sun's bounty, and where the energy of flowing water is harnessed without harm to ecosystems. Could this vision of clean, renewable energy fuel not just our homes but also a revolution in thought?

Now, imagine the ripple effects of environmental kindness on human health and happiness. Parks and green spaces are not mere decorations but vital organs of urban life, places for recreation and reprieve. How might our physical and mental well-being improve if we cultivate a deeper connection with the natural world, even in the city's heart?

In the depths of the ocean, imagine a coral reef vibrant and teeming with life, a kaleidoscope of colours and shapes. Fishing practices that respect the balance of marine ecosystems ensure the abundance of these underwater wonders for generations. Can you see the wisdom in preserving the beauty of the deep, recognizing its role in the grand tapestry of life?

And what of the air we breathe? Imagine a world where the skies are clear, where children grow up without the threat of pollution-induced asthma. Clean air is not a luxury but a right, safeguarded by policies and practices that prioritize health and sustainability. Could we commit to such a vision, recognizing that the air we share connects us all?

Imagine a legacy of kindness towards the environment, where each of us is a guardian of the Earth. In every decision, let us consider the impact on the natural world, from the products we buy to the food we eat. In this way, kindness becomes not just an act but a way of life, an ethos that guides us toward a more sustainable future.

Can you envision a time when the environment no longer needs protecting because our respect for it is inherent in every action we take? This is the world we must aspire to, a world where kindness towards the Earth is as natural as the ebb and flow of the tides, as instinctive as the return of birds with the changing seasons.

Let us imagine, then, not as a mere exercise in thought but as a prelude to action. For in the power of our collective imagination lies the first step toward creating a reality where the environment is cherished, where kindness is cultivated, and where the Earth thrives alongside humanity.

So, let us not merely close our eyes to imagine. Let us open our hearts to feel, our minds to dream, and our hands to build. Imagine cultivating kindness towards the environment—now let us bring that vision to life.

Imagine Embracing Biophilia: Love of Nature

In the heart of a dense forest, where the air is alive with the whispers of leaves, imagine yourself standing still. The dappled sunlight dances across the mossy floor, painting patterns of light and shadow. Can you feel the pulse of the Earth beneath your feet, the steady rhythm of life that courses through the veins of every tree and stone?

The concept of biophilia suggests that we humans have an innate love for nature and a longing to connect with the living world. It is this deep-seated bond that calls us to the wild places, to the untamed edges of our existence. But what if this connection goes beyond mere affinity? What if it is a fundamental part of our being, essential for our physical and emotional well-being?

Imagine a life where our homes are extensions of the natural world, where walls of greenery breathe life into our spaces. Picture windows that frame the ever-changing artistry of nature, where every glance outside is a reminder of the beauty that thrives beyond our own creations. Can you envision architecture that doesn't just stand on the land but converses with it, buildings that give more than they take, that nurture as they shelter?

Delve into the details of such a life. In the corners of each room, potted plants offer more than just aesthetic pleasure—they cleanse the air, and they bring a fragment of the forest into our daily routines. The materials we use in our homes could be sourced responsibly, with a mindfulness that honours the resources given by the Earth.

Pause for a moment. Reflect on the sounds of nature: the rustling of leaves, the babbling of brooks, the chorus of birdsong at dawn. How often do we allow these simple melodies to permeate the walls we've built around ourselves? Imagine if our days were scored by this natural symphony, a soundtrack that reminds us of the life that thrives just beyond our reach.

Consider the nourishment we derive from the Earth. Every morsel of food is a gift, a result of the intricate dance between soil, water, and sun. Imagine if we cultivated our food with a reverence for this process, with gardens that are not just plots of land but sanctuaries where plants grow robust and resilient. Can you taste the difference in a vegetable that has been tended with love, that carries within it the essence of the sun and the care of a human hand?

Imagine children growing up with dirt under their fingernails, with knees stained green from the grass. Playgrounds mimic the uneven terrain of the wild, where young minds learn agility not on plastic and metal but on logs, stones, and earth. What lessons could be ingrained when play and exploration are rooted in the natural world?

Now, imagine the healing power of nature. Think of hospitals and healing centres designed with gardens and natural light, where recovery is supported by views of the sky and access to fresh air. Consider the impact on health when environments are created with an understanding of biophilia—spaces that are not sterile and closed off but that breathe and bloom and inspire wellness.

In the workplace, picture desks are positioned to catch the morning light, offices are punctuated with plant life, and meetings are held on walking trails surrounded by the serenity of greenery. How might productivity and creativity flourish when the barriers between indoors and out are softened when the stifling air of conventional workspaces is replaced with the freshness of the natural world?

Imagine our cities and towns as ecosystems in their own right, where urban planning is done with a consciousness of wildlife corridors and native species. Picture streets lined with trees that bear fruit and offer shade, where every turn reveals a pocket park or a vertical garden clinging to a building's facade. Could this be the fabric of a community that celebrates its place within the greater ecosystem?

Imagine the joy that could flood our lives if we were to truly embrace biophilia, to recognize our love for nature not as a luxury but as a necessity. Imagine how our daily choices might shift if we were to see ourselves as part of the web of life, interconnected and interdependent. What transformations might unfold if the love of nature were woven into every aspect of our existence?

Imagine, then, taking a deep breath of air rich with the scent of rain and soil. Imagine your heart opening wide to the beauty and complexity of the natural world. This is the essence of biophilia, a call to renew our bond with the Earth. It is an invitation to live in harmony, to find our place in the circle of life, and to nurture the planet that nurtures us in return.

Let us not just imagine. Let us act. Let us cultivate our biophilic instincts and allow them to guide our steps. In a world that often feels disconnected, let us be the ones to weave the threads of nature back into the tapestry of our lives. Embrace biophilia and love of nature, and watch as the world transforms before your eyes—lush, vibrant, and alive with possibility.

www.ingramcontent.com/pod-product-compliance
Lightning Source LLC
Chambersburg PA
CBHW051303120626
46547CB00015B/2069